# Learning to Pass

# ECDL
## Practice Exercises

## Angela Bessant

**www.heinemann.co.uk**
✓ Free online support
✓ Useful weblinks
✓ 24 hour online ordering

**01865 888058**

**Heinemann**
*Inspiring generations*

# Heinemann

Heinemann is an imprint of Pearson Education Limited, a company incorporated
in England and Wales, having its registered office at Edinburgh Gate, Harlow, Essex, CM20 2JE.
Registered company number: 872828

Heinemann is the registered trademark of Harcourt Education Limited

© Angela Bessant, 2006

First published 2006

10  09  08
10 9 8 7 6 5 4 3

British Library Cataloguing in Publication Data is available
from the British Library on request.

13-digit ISBN: 978 0 435578 39 8

Edited by
Designed by [select form dropdown]
Typeset by [select form dropdown]
Produced by [select form dropdown]

Original illustrations © Pearson Education Limited, 2006

Printed in Great Britain by Ashford Colour Press Ltd, Gosport, Hants

Cover photo: © Corbis

## Acknowledgements

This book and CD would not have been produced without the help and encouragement of a great many
people and I would like to express my profound thanks to all of them. At Heinemann, above all I would like
to thank Nick Starren for his professionalism and support at the many milestones of production and Elaine
Tuffery for kindly commissioning this resource. A big thank you is due to all learners, tutors and colleagues
whose critical comments always add more clarity to the work. Thanks to the Institute of IT Training, the ECDL
Foundation and the British Computer Society. And finally, I would like to thank my family, and in particular
Mike, for his indispensable help with the theoretical sections.

The author would like to thank Gemma Bessant for supplying the artwork for model1.gif and hare and
tortoise (Exercise 23, Module 3).

Every effort has been made to contact copyright holders of material reproduced in this book. Any omissions
will be rectified in subsequent printings if notice is given to the publishers.

Microsoft product screen shots reprinted with permission from Microsoft Corporation.

## Websites

Please note that the examples of websites suggested in this book were up to date at the time of writing. It is
essential for tutors to preview each site before using it to ensure that the URL is still accurate and the content
is appropriate. We suggest that tutors bookmark useful sites and consider enabling students to access them
through the school or college intranet.

Tel: 01865 888058 www.heinemann.co.uk

# Contents

# Contents

# Introduction

In order to become proficient in using a computer and to pass the European Computer Driving Licence (ECDL) tests it is necessary to practise. In this way you will consolidate your understanding and build up your confidence. This book provides lots of activities for you to do just that. It covers all seven modules for Version 4 of the ECDL syllabus and also contains an additional module, 'Using IT', which forms part of the BCS IT User qualification Level 2.

The book format closely follows that of the *Learning to Pass ECDL* books, where all the knowledge and skills are covered in detail. Skills are listed at the top of the exercises in which they first appear. The book has been produced using MS Office 2003 and Windows XP but in most cases is compatible with some earlier versions of Office. The CD-ROM contains all the source files necessary to complete the tasks (thus saving lots of laborious keying-in time and leaving you free to concentrate on other skills). Sample answers to exercises in Modules 3, 4, 5, and 6 are provided. Answers are also provided for the multiple-choice questions and crosswords. *Note*: The tasks in this book are only *practice* tasks. Successful completion does not imply certification of the module by the ECDL Foundation.

See the following websites for more information on the ECDL syllabus, tests and test centres and the BCS IT User qualification:

www.bcsituser.org
www.ecdl.co.uk
www.ecdl.com

Contact:
ECDL
The British Computer Society
1 Sandford Street
Swindon
Wiltshire SN1 1HJ

For a mapping grid for each unit to the ECDL Syllabus 4 visit www.heinemann.co.uk/ecdlmap and click on Free User Support, then ECDL Practice Exercises Mapping Document.

Visit the Angela Bessant forum on www.bessant.co.uk/forum

Visit the Heinemann website for details of other ECDL materials (including the *Learning to Pass ECDL* books and CDs), errata, additional materials and updates: www.heinemann.co.uk

## Limit of liability/disclaimer of warranty

The accuracy and completeness of the information provided herein are not guaranteed or warranted to produce any particular results and the advice and strategies contained herein may not be suitable for every individual.

# About the CD-ROM

The CD-ROM contains source files for the exercises (instructions of how to copy these files to your own storage medium are given below). Sample answers for Modules 3, 4, 5 and 6 as well as crossword solutions and answers to multiple-choice questions can also be found on the CD-ROM. These are in PDF format and can be accessed as shown below. *Note*: If you do not have Acrobat Reader on your computer, it can be downloaded for free from the Internet.

## Accessing the answers to exercises

1   Load Acrobat Reader.
2   From the **File** menu, select **Open**.
3   Select the location from where you want to open the file.
4   With the file selected, click on **Open**.

## Printing the answers to exercises

1   From the **File** menu, select **Print**.
2   A Print dialogue box is displayed with a number of different options.
3   Make any changes to the printing options as required.
4   Check that the correct printer is selected and click on **OK**.

## Copying a file from the CD-ROM

1   Press the button on the CD-ROM drive to access the CD tray.
2   Place the CD-ROM in the tray with the label uppermost (i.e. showing).
3   Push the tray in to close it.
4   On the Windows XP desktop, from the **Start** menu, select **Run**. The **Run** dialogue box is displayed.
5   In the **Run** box, key in the name of the CD drive. *Note:* This is usually drive D or E so key in **D:** (or **E:**).
6   Click on **OK**.
7   The contents of the CD-ROM are displayed.
8   Locate the relevant file. (If the file is contained in a folder, you will need to open that folder by double-clicking on it.) See below if you want to select multiple files or the entire contents of the CD-ROM.
9   Select **Copy this file** from the **File and Folder Tasks** list.
10   In the **Copy Items** box, click on the destination drive.
11   Click on **Copy**.

## Copying more than one file from the CD-ROM

Follow the steps above except:

- At step 8, select multiple files by holding down the **Shift** key while clicking on adjacent files or the **Ctrl** key while clicking on non-adjacent files.
- At step 9, select **Copy the selected items**.

## Copying entire contents

Follow the steps above except:

- At step 8, from the **Edit** menu, select **Select All**.

## Copying Access database files

1  Copy the files onto your hard disk (as above).
2  Before you open each file, in My Computer or Windows Explorer, right-click on the file and select **Properties** at the bottom of the drop-down list.
3  With the **General** tab selected, in the **Attributes** section, click in the **Read-only** box to remove the tick.
4  Click on **Apply**, then on **OK**.

# Concepts of Information Technology (IT)

**Module 1**

## Section

**1** General questions

**2** Multiple-choice questions

**3** Crossword

*Note:* Answers to the Multiple-choice questions and Crossword sections can be found on the CD-ROM.

1

# Section 1 *General questions*

## Exercise 1

1 Name two government organisations that might use a mainframe computer.

2 What types of removable computer memory would be best suited to storing colour images from a digital camera?

3 Explain the difference between these networks: an extranet and an intranet.

4 Why do the majority of PDAs not use a hard disk?

5 List the main reasons for keeping backup copies of your computer files.

6 Describe the basic precautions necessary to restrict unauthorised access to computer data.

7 Explain the differences between shareware and public domain software.

8 Describe measures that will reduce the risk of infecting your computer with a virus.

9 What equipment and facilities would you need to access the Internet using a home computer?

10 Explain why the amount of RAM may affect the performance of a computer.

## Exercise 2

1 Which type of monitor (CRT or flatscreen) uses the least energy? Name the related software feature that provides further energy saving.

2 Why should computer hardware and consumables be professionally disposed of or recycled?

3 Describe some advantages and disadvantages associated with using telecommunications to work from home.

4 What do the initials HASAW stand for and how does this legislation relate to computers?

5 Describe the key stages in the development of a computer-based system.

6 What is a graphical user interface (GUI)? Describe some of the advantages of this software design approach.

7 List the three main components of a desktop computer system.

8 What is the most common unit of storage for a modern hard disk: megabyte, gigabyte or terabyte?

9 Compared with an older film camera, what advantages and disadvantages might a digital camera have?

10 Which are the most appropriate applications software packages to use for the following tasks?

    a Editing images.

    b Calculating expenditure.

    c Producing a brochure.

    d Producing a letter.

    e Filing customer details.

    f Searching for information on the Internet.

## Exercise 3

1 How could you participate in e-commerce and what might be the advantages and disadvantages of electronic transactions?

2 What precautions should you take before purchasing from a website?

3 Name three input and three output computer devices.

4 For mobile work, what advantages does a PDA have when compared with a laptop?

5 Why might stored data be corrupted when an operating computer is moved?

6 Name two types of computer virus.

7 Describe the purpose of the Data Protection Act.

8 Name two government organisations that routinely exchange data.

9 What steps can be taken to minimise the risk of purchasing pirated software?

10 Explain the term asymmetric digital subscriber line (ADSL). What is the main benefit of ADSL when accessing the Internet from home?

11 Name the most popular service available on the Internet.

# Section 2 *Multiple-choice questions*

**1** What is the name given to the physical devices that make up a computer system?

   **a** Software.

   **b** Network.

   **c** Hardware.

   **d** Documentation.

**2** Which type of input/output device is used by a PDA?

   **a** CRT monitor.

   **b** Touch screen.

   **c** Flatscreen monitor.

   **d** Keyboard.

**3** Which type of storage is best suited to backing up full-screen colour pictures?

   **a** Floppy disk.

   **b** RAM.

   **c** Hard disk.

   **d** CD-ROM.

**4** Which of the following devices allows computers to communicate over the telephone system?

   **a** Modem.

   **b** Speaker.

   **c** Mouse.

   **d** Microphone.

**5** What application would be used to look for information on the Internet?

   **a** Database.

   **b** Spreadsheet.

   **c** Web browser.

   **d** Presentation.

**6** Which of the following devices is able to convert printed text or images into signals that a computer can understand?

   **a** Mouse.

   **b** Joystick.

   **c** Lightpen.

   **d** Scanner.

**7** The speed of the CPU used in modern laptop computers is measured in:

   **a** Kilohertz (KHz).

   **b** Megabytes (MB).

   **c** Gigahertz (GHz).

   **d** Gigabytes (GB).

**8** Who would be the most likely to operate a mainframe computer system?

   **a** A primary school.

   **b** An insurance company.

   **c** A doctor's surgery.

   **d** A home worker.

**9** The rules governing the supply and storage of computer-held information are covered in the UK by the:

   **a** Data Protection Act.

   **b** Health and Safety Act.

   **c** Copyright Protection Act.

   **d** Employment Act.

**10** Which of the following could be associated with a computer virus?

   **a** Race horse.

   **b** Trojan horse.

   **c** Rocking horse.

   **d** Clothes horse.

**11** When purchasing goods via the Internet, which symbol denotes that you are entering a secure site?

   **a** Open padlock.

   **b** Encryption key.

   **c** Magnifying glass.

   **d** Closed padlock.

1

**12** What is the primary role of a programmer in a computer development team?

   **a** Hardware design.

   **b** Marketing.

   **c** Software design.

   **d** Project management.

**13** Which category of software has the least restrictions on copying and distribution?

   **a** Shareware.

   **b** Copyright.

   **c** Freeware.

   **d** Public domain.

**14** The possibility of sustaining repetitive strain injury (RSI) is mainly reduced by:

   **a** Using a higher-performance PC.

   **b** Keeping wrists level with keyboard.

   **c** Leaving windows open.

   **d** Drinking cold coffee.

**15** Which type of computer is *least* at risk from unauthorised data access?

   **a** Standalone desktop.

   **b** Portable Digital Assistant (PDA).

   **c** Laptop.

   **d** Networked desktop.

# Section 3  *Crossword*

**Across**

2 Very high-performance computer (9)

4 'Brain' of PC (14)

5 Software protection that needs a key (10)

8 Form of working from home (11)

10 Enables computers to communicate via telephone network (5)

12 Input device that cats shouldn't eat (5)

16 Inputs printed text and images (7)

20 Law that prohibits illegal copying (9)

23 The R in RSI (10)

24 Make these frequently (7)

25 Removable 3.5-inch magnetic disk (8)

**Down**

1 You should never write this down (8)

3 Improve by opening windows (11)

4 Device that can input sound to computer (10)

6 Type of volatile memory (1, 1, 1)

7 Works like an upside-down mouse (7, 4)

9 Lower-power alternative to a CRT monitor (10)

11 Application designed to store and search for information (8)

13 Output device that may use inkjet or laser technology (7)

14 An internal website (8)

15 A designer of software (10)

17 Computer for the top of your knees (6)

18 Application that combines filing and calculator functions (11)

19 Computer problem (3)

21 Can make a computer very unwell (5)

22 Type of removable disk that sounds fast (3)

# Using the computer and managing files

## Section

Please note that many skills are expanded upon and duplicated throughout the exercises.

# Section 1 *Getting started*

### Exercise 1

**1** Explain the correct routine for starting the computer.

**2** Explain the correct routine for shutting down the computer. Why is it important to shut down the computer using the correct procedure?

**3** Explain what you would do if you had a non-responding application.

**4** Explain how to reduce/enlarge an application window.

**5** How do you move windows on the desktop?

**6** Name the following items and explain what they are for.

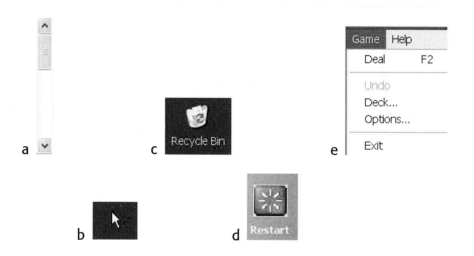

**7** When using the mouse what is meant by the following terms?
   **a** Click.
   **b** Double-click.
   **c** Drag and drop.
   **d** Hover.

**8** Identify these items in the screenshot below: **Title bar, Menu bar, Close** button, **Minimize** button.

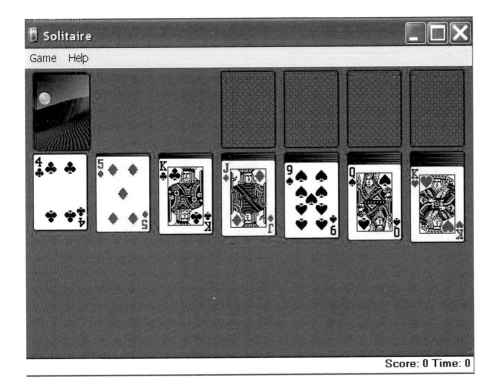

**9** What is the **Start** button used for?

**10** Search Windows Help to find out how to set a screen saver.

# Section 2 *Working with icons*

## Exercise 2

1  View your computer's system information and answer the following:

    a  What is the operating system on your computer?

    b  What version number is it?

    c  How much RAM is installed?

2  How do you access the **Control Panel**? What is it for?

3  Explain how to do the following:

    • set your computer's time and date
    • change the desktop background
    • change the colour settings and resolution
    • apply a screensaver
    • change the keyboard language
    • change the sound settings.

4  What does the **Print Screen** key do?

5  Create a desktop shortcut for the **Calculator** (usually found in **All Programs, Accessories**).

6  Add the **Paint** program (usually found in **All Programs, Accessories**) to the **Start** menu. How do you remove programs from the **Start** menu?

7  Identify the following desktop icons: file, folder, application shortcut.

8  How do you move desktop icons?

9  How do you Auto Arrange desktop icons?

10  How do you open a file/folder/application from the desktop?

11  Explain how you would install a software application. Explain how you would uninstall a software application.

# Section 3  *Working with files and folders*

## Exercise 3

**1**  A diskette (floppy disk) is a device used to store files. Which of the following are also used to store files?

    **a**  CD-ROM.

    **b**  Hard disk.

    **c**  Mouse.

    **d**  Network drive.

    **e**  Keyboard.

**2**  How can you access and view the drives, folders and files on your computer? Explain the hierarchical structure for computer storage.

**3**  How do you display folder/file properties?

**4**  Why is it important to maintain correct file extensions when renaming files? What file types are denoted by the extensions in the list below? (Please photocopy this page and fill in the photocopied table.)

| | |
|---|---|
| .xls | |
| .mdb | |
| .ppt | |
| .bmp | |
| .rtf | |
| .txt | |
| .htm | |
| .mp3 | |
| .wav .au | |
| .zip | |
| .pdf | |
| .tmp | |
| .gif .jpg .tif | |
| .exe | |
| .mpeg .avi | |

**2**

5 Why is it important to make backup copies of files? Where would you store backup files and why?

6 Explain how to format a disk.

7 What does file compression mean?

8 How can you view a list of recently used files?

## Exercise 4 (practical)

*Skills*
- Select a file(s)/folder(s)
- Change file status: read-only, read/write
- Create a new folder and subfolder
- Rename a file/folder
- Delete a file/folder
- Sort files by name, size, type, date modified
- Empty the **Recycle Bin**
- Restore a file/folder from the **Recycle Bin**
- Copy a file/folder
- Move a file/folder

Folder required: **Ex4 mod2**

1 Empty the **Recycle Bin**.

2 In the folder **Ex4 mod2**, create a folder with the name **practice**.

3 Create two subfolders, with the names **trial1** and **trial2**, in the newly created **practice** folder.

4 Copy all files with the extension .ppt in the **comp2** folder to **comp3/Homer**.

5 In the **comp1** folder, sort the files by name.

6 In the **comp2** folder, sort the files by ascending order of date modified.

7 In the **comp3/Homer** folder, sort the files by size.

8 Delete the file **travel.mdb** from the **comp2** folder.

9 Move the smallest file in the **comp1/ang1** folder to the **trial2** folder (created in step 3).

10 In the **comp3/Homer** folder, change the attribute of the **swimming.ppt** file to Read-only.

11 Change the attribute of the **comp4/max** folder to Read/write.

**12**  Rename the **comp1** folder **Ang files**.

**13**  Rename the file **earth.doc** in the **comp2** folder **planet.doc**.

**14**  Restore the file **travel.mdb** from the **Recycle Bin**.

**15**  In the **Ang files** folder, select the folder **ang** and the files **trail** and **history** and copy them to the **trial2 folder**.

**16**  Copy the folders **Ang files** and **comp2** to the **trial1** folder.

**17**  Move the folder **comp3** to the **trial2** folder.

**18**  In the **trial2** folder, sort the files by type.

## Exercise 5 (practical)

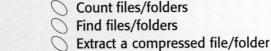

*Skills*
- Count files/folders
- Find files/folders
- Extract a compressed file/folder
- Compress a file/folder

Folder required: **Ex5 mod2**

**1**  Find all the files with the extension .xls in the **Ex5 mod2** folder (include all subfolders) and make a note of the number found.

**2**  Copy all the files with the extension .jpg from **comp6/large** to **comp8/ Manchester**.

**3**  In the **Ex5 mod2** folder, how many files and folders are there with the text 'right' in the filename? Note down the answer.

**4**  Compress the file **summer.jpg** in the **comp8/Leeds** folder and save it to a floppy disk.

**5**  Extract any compressed files in **comp8/sports**.

## Exercise 6

**1**  What is a computer virus?

**2**  How can a virus be transmitted to a computer?

**3**  What problems can a virus cause?

**4** What software can you use to help ensure that your computer remains virus free?

**5** What does 'disinfecting' mean in relation to virus scanning?

**6** Ideally how often should you update anti-virus software?

    **a** Once every 5 years.

    **b** Never.

    **c** Every summer.

    **d** On a regular basis.

**7** Explain how you might use a typical anti-virus software application.

# Section 4  *Using and printing from a text-editing application*

## Exercise 7 (practical)

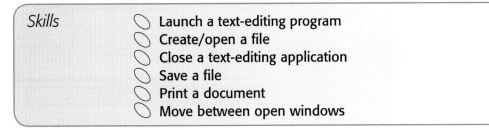

*Skills*  Launch a text-editing program
Create/open a file
Close a text-editing application
Save a file
Print a document
Move between open windows

Folder required: **Ex7 mod2**

**1**  Open a text-editing program (e.g. Notepad).

**2**  Create an 'answer' file by keying in your name and today's date and the heading **Module 2 Practice**. This file will be referred to as your **Answer** file.

**3**  Using **Windows Help**, find some information about changing the time on your computer.

**4**  Using copy and paste, copy a few lines from the **Help** topic just found in step 3 to your **Answer** file.

**5**  Count the number of files in the **Ex7 mod2** folder and key in the answer on the next line of your **Answer** file.

**6**  Save and print the **Answer** file.

## Exercise 8

**1**  Explain how you would change the default printer from the list of those already installed.

**2**  Explain how to add a new printer on the computer.

**3**  How do you view a print job's progress using a desktop print manager?

**4** You have started to print several documents. How would you do the following?

   **a** Pause printing.

   **b** Delete a print job.

   **c** Restart printing after pausing.

**5** In the screenshot below, identify the following: toolbar, status bar, default printer.

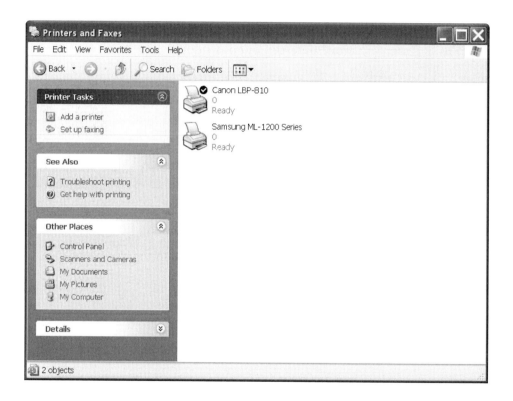

# Word processing

**Module 3**

## Section

Please note that many skills are expanded upon and duplicated throughout the exercises.

3

# Section 1 *Getting started*

## Exercise 1

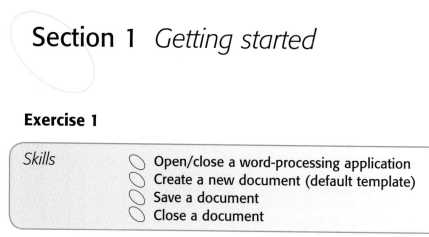

*Skills*
- ○ Open/close a word-processing application
- ○ Create a new document (default template)
- ○ Save a document
- ○ Close a document

**1** Open your word-processing application and enter the following text on a blank page:

Bores occur at different places throughout the world (I am not referring to the human variety here!). I am referring to the natural occurrence of a surge wave that forms in a funnel-shaped estuary.

Britain has the phenomenal Severn Bore that can be seen in the tidal estuary of the River Severn. The estuary narrows to 5 miles wide at Avonmouth, to only 1 mile at Sharpness and less than 100 yards at Minsterworth. Not only does the width of the river decrease rapidly but so does its depth. The incoming tide is funnelled into an ever-decreasing channel and so the surge wave is formed.

Bore surfing is an awesome experience. It is also extremely dangerous and requires extensive experience and understanding of the tides. It is essential to obtain expert tuition and advice before taking to the water.

**2** Save the text with the filename **severn(yr initials)**.

**3** Close the file and exit the application.

## Exercise 2

**1** Open your word-processing application and enter the following text on a blank page:

COMPETITION TIME

Starlings are widespread in the UK and most people will have seen them at some time or other. The starling lives in open woodland, hedgerows, parks and gardens. Starlings are smaller than blackbirds and look black in colour, but when seen close up you will notice that they have a green and purple sheen. They are not considered to be everyone's favourite bird due to their aggressive and gregarious nature, often pushing other birds out of the way when feeding at bird tables.

They can be seen all year round in the UK since they spend the winters here. During the winter they live in flocks. In the late afternoon, flocks join together as they move towards the night-time roost. It is a most spectacular sight as they whirl and spin in a cloud-like formation.

To enter this month's competition, we are looking for the best starling photo. We have a £20 voucher for the best entry, and a 50% discount voucher for our book of the month for 5 runners-up. Please e-mail your entry to us at the usual address.

Be quick! Entries must be received by the last Friday of this month.

**2**  Save the text with the filename **comp(yr initials)**.

**3**  Close the file and exit the application.

**3**

# Section 2 *Editing and printing*

### Exercise 3

| *Skills* | ○ Open an existing document |
|---|---|
| | ○ Add text |
| | ○ Spellcheck and make changes where necessary |
| | ○ Resave a previously saved file |
| | ○ Preview and print a document |
| | ○ Save a document under another name |

Files required: **comp(yr initials)** (saved in Exercise 2)
**severn(yr initials)** (saved in Exercise 1)

1  Open the file **comp(yr initials)**.

2  Add your name at the end of the document.

3  Save the document as **comp1(yr initials)**.

4  Proofread, spellcheck and make changes where necessary.

5  Resave the file with the same name as that given in step 3.

6  Preview and print the document.

7  Close the file.

8  Open the file **severn(yr initials)** saved in Exercise 1.

9  Spellcheck and resave.

10  Preview and print on A4 paper, portrait display.

11  Close the file.

## Exercise 4

> *Skills*
> ◯ Display/hide non-printing characters
> ◯ Use zoom tool
> ◯ Add words to a custom dictionary
> ◯ Print: change display orientation, selection

Files required: **sudoku.doc**

1  Open the file **sudoku.doc** and save it with the name **sudoku(yr initials)**.

2  Zoom the document down to 100%.

3  Hide all non-printing characters.

4  Add the word **Sudoku** to the custom dictionary and perform a spellcheck and make changes where necessary.

5  Add your name on the line directly under the heading and underline it.

6  Resave the document.

7  Print the document.

8  Print only the first paragraph including the heading and your name in landscape display.

9  Close the file.

**3**

## Exercise 5

> *Skills*
> ◯ Insert/delete text
> ◯ Overwrite text
> ◯ Replace words with other words

Files required: **question.doc**

1  Open the file **question.doc**.

2  Add your name to the end of the document and save as **quest1**.

3  Insert the following sentences in the fourth paragraph after the sentence ending... **saving on your next holiday**.

Note that this offer is valid for a limited period only. You must act within 28 days.

**4**   Replace the word **constantly** with **continually**.

**5**   In the second paragraph, second sentence, overwrite the words **will do our best to exceed** with **endeavour to meet**.

**6**   In the second paragraph, first sentence, delete the word **our** after the word **improve**.

**7**   Delete the final sentence, i.e. **We look forward to hearing from you soon.**

**8**   Quick save the document, print and close.


## Exercise 6

| Skills | |
| --- | --- |
| | ○ Insert a new paragraph |
| | ○ Join paragraphs |
| | ○ Change margins |

Files required: **prepvenue.doc**

**1**   Open the file **prepvenue.doc**.

**2**   Add your name to the end of the document and save as **prep1**.

**3**   Create a new paragraph at the text beginning **It is advisable**… and create a new paragraph at the text beginning **Ensure the venue for**…
Join the paragraph beginning **Check the possibility**… to the previous paragraph ending… **for an event**.

**4**   Insert the following paragraph after the paragraph ending… **with the technology**.

Ensure that the venue is suitably laid out so that you can stand beside your lecture materials so avoiding having to turn your back on the audience. Check that everyone can see the slides and that the text is large enough to be read from all parts of the room.

**5**   Select all the text in the document and apply 5 pt spacing above and below each paragraph.

**6**   Change the left and right margins to 2 cm.

**7**   Save the document as **prep2** and print.

**8**   Close the file.

# Exercise 7

*Skills*
- Copy/move text within a document
- Copy/move text to another document
- Open several documents
- Switch between open documents
- Use the **Find** command

Files required: **hols.doc**
**cornwall.doc**

1 Open the file **hols.doc**.

2 Select the third paragraph beginning: **Our properties vary in size**... and move it so that it appears beneath the heading **PROPERTIES AVAILABLE**. (Leave a line space between this heading and the moved paragraph.)

3 Open the file **cornwall.doc**, select all of the text and copy it to the **hols.doc** file so that it forms the end of the second paragraph, i.e. after the text... **more experienced climber**. Save the **hols.doc** file as **hols1**.

4 Switch to the **cornwall.doc** file, spellcheck and save as **corn1**.

5 Switch to the **hols1.doc**. Use the **Find** command to find the word **Tintagel** and change it to **Boscastle**.

6 Spellcheck the **hols1** document and quick save it.

7 Print the **hols1** document and close.

8 Print the **corn1** document and close.

# Exercise 8

*Skills*
- Insert special characters/symbols

1 Open a new file and enter the following text:

Sometimes when copying information you will come across symbols and special characters. Have a go at inserting the following special characters: © and ®. Now try inserting the following symbols: ✂ ☎ ☺ ✿ ↘ ☹ €.

There are accented letters in foreign languages. These words are Spanish: cumpleaños, espantapájaros, cortacésped. These words are German: für, Universität, schön. These words are French: février, élève, garçon, août

**2**   Save the file with the name **special**.

**3**   Change the left and right margins to 5 cm.

**4**   Change the top and bottom margins to 3 cm.

**5**   Print in landscape.

**6**   Close the file.

# Section 3 *Formatting*

## Exercise 9

> *Skills*
> - Centre
> - Embolden
> - Italicise
> - Underline
> - Change case

Files required: **languages.doc**

**1** Open the file **languages.doc**, add your name at the end and save the document as **lang1**.

**2** Use the **Change Case** option to change the heading to upper case.

**3** Centre the heading.

**4** In the final sentence, change the format of the words **French**, **German**, **Spanish**, **Welsh** and **Italian** to bold and underlined.

**5** Italicise the word **Germanic** in the first sentence.

**6** In the third paragraph, final sentence, underline the words **grammar** and **vocabulary**.

**7** Resave the document, print and close the file.

## Exercise 10

> *Skills*
> - Apply colours to text
> - Change font type and font size
> - Copy formatting
> - Insert/remove paragraph marks

Files required: **structure.doc**

**1** Open the file **structure.doc** and remove the paragraph marks.

**2** Add your name at the end and save as **structure1**.

**3** Apply the colour *Dark Teal* to the heading **Structuring Your Presentation**.

**4** Change the font of the first paragraph to Arial, 14 pt.

**5** Copy the format of the word **visually** in the last sentence of the second paragraph to the text **visuals** in the final sentence of the third paragraph.

**6** Move the second paragraph so that it becomes the final paragraph.

**7** Set the top margin to 5 cm.

**8** Resave the document, print and close the file.

## Exercise 11

| Skills | |
|---|---|
| | ○ **Change line spacing** |
| | ○ **Control justification/alignment** |
| | ○ **Control hyphenation** |

Files required: **structure1** (saved in Exercise 10)

**1** Open the file **structure1** and save it with the name **struc2**.

**2** Select the heading and first paragraph and set the line spacing to double.

**3** Apply 8 pt spacing between the second and third paragraphs.

**4** Centre-align the heading.

**5** Change the left margin to 4 cm and the right margin to 2 cm.

**6** Justify the document (excluding the heading) using automatic hyphenation.

**7** Save as **struc3**, print and close.

## Exercise 12

| Skills | |
|---|---|
| | ○ **Indent text** |
| | ○ **Use and change pagination** |
| | ○ **Print specific pages** |

Files required: **adventure.doc**

**1** Open the file **adventure.doc** and resave as **holspages**.

**2** Print only page 2.

**3**  Enter the heading **Activity Adventures** and format to 16 pt, Arial font and underline.

**4**  Find and replace all occurrences of the text **Naturetrail Holidays** with **Activity Adventures**.

**5**  Indent the first paragraph by 3 cm from the left and right margins.

**6**  Create a first-line indent of 2 cm in the second paragraph.

**7**  Create a hanging indent of 1.5 cm in the final paragraph before **DON'T DELAY – BOOK TODAY**.

**8**  Insert a page break before the **PRICES** heading.

**9**  Delete the page break before the **HOW TO BOOK** heading.

**10**  Add the following text at the end of the document:

**ACTIVITY ADVENTURES ©**
**Amended by (Your name)**

**11**  Insert automatic page numbers at the bottom centre. Show the page number on the first page.

**12**  Save as **adventure1**, print and close.

## Exercise 13

| *Skills* | ◌ Apply Headers and Footers |
|---|---|
|  | ◌ Format superscript/subscript |

**1**  Open a new file and enter the following text:

### Animals and Water

Water's chemical description is $H_2O$. Many animals are able to survive on very little water. Perhaps the best example is the camel. The camel uses its hump not as a store for water but as a store of fat that it can convert into water. In fact it can go for 17 days without a drink. Camels can drink large amounts of water, up to 20 gallons at a time! It is able to store this water in its bloodstream.

The koala gets its name from an ancient Aboriginal word meaning 'no drink'. In fact it only drinks when ill or when there is not enough moisture in the Eucalyptus leaves that form its staple diet.

$H_2O$ facts

Humans are 50–60% water
Frogs are 78% water
Jellyfish are 95% water

**2**  Proofread and spellcheck your work and save as **water.doc**.

**3**  Apply a header in size 10 pt to display **Water**, an automatic today's date, and an automatic filename.

**4**  Resave, print and close.

**5**  Open a new file and enter the following text:

*Squares*

The first five square numbers are 1, 4, 9, 16, 25…

Each of these square numbers is the result of multiplying it by itself…

1 x 1, 2 x 2, 3 x 3, 4 x 4, 5 x 5…

These can also be written down (where the superscript $^2$ means squared)…

$1^2$, $2^2$, $3^2$, $4^2$, $5^2$…

**6**  Apply a Footer in 12 pt to display your name and the page number at the right.

**7**  Proofread and spellcheck your work and then save as **square.doc**.

**8**  Print and close.

# Section 4 *More formatting*

## Exercise 14

| *Skills* | ◯ Use bulleted lists |
|---|---|
| | ◯ Use numbered lists |
| | ◯ Add borders/shading |

Files required: **lists.doc**

**1** Open the file **lists.doc**.

**2** Remove the bullets from the list of days.

**3** Apply bullets to the three lines listed beginning **Maintaining**…

**4** Set the bullets in the above list to display as ticks ✓.

**5** In the final sentence, make the items that follow into a numbered list:

**Inform the audience of what you are going to tell them**
**Present the information**
**End the presentation by summarising the main message again**

**6** Add a Box border to the above list.

**7** Add the following text at the end of the document and make into a bulleted list (do not use a bullet next to the heading **General**):

*General*
**Try to create a memorable atmosphere.**
**Alter the tone of your voice to add interest.**
**Use first-hand experience so that the audience gets to know a little about you.**

**8** Add a top and bottom Box border and shading to the text just entered.

**9** Proofread and spellcheck your work and save as **mylists**.

**10** Print and close.

**3**

## Exercise 15

**1** Open a new file and enter the following text (use tabs to create the listed items):

Vitamin C is an essential vitamin for human life. It is also known as ascorbic acid. Different vitamins are required by the body. These are obtained from foods, drinks and some are also produced within the body, for example, vitamin D is produced when we are out in the sunshine and take in the ultraviolet radiation on our skin.

Vitamin C is a water-soluble vitamin and is not usually associated with toxicity, as is the case with some other vitamins when taken in large doses. A deficiency in vitamin C can result in the disease scurvy. Scurvy causes problems with gums, leaving them bleeding and inflamed. Its other symptoms are pain in the joints and muscle wasting.

Vitamin C is found in citrus fruits including oranges, blackcurrants and limes. In fact British navy men took lime juice on long sea expeditions to ward off scurvy and were nicknamed 'Limeys'. Vitamin C is also found in vegetables, such as tomatoes and green leafy vegetables.

The following list provides a useful guide.

| Fruit | Vit C/100g | Value |
|---|---|---|
| Apple | 6 | quite good |
| Banana | 9 | good |
| Kiwifruit | 98 | exceptional |
| Grapefruit | 34 | excellent |
| Orange | 53 | excellent |

**2** Save as **vitamins.doc**.

**3** Proofread and spellcheck.

**4** Ensure that the first three paragraphs only are fully justified.

**5** Resave, print and close.

**6** Open a new file and enter the following using centre tabs and decimal tabs.

| Coffee | 0.95 |
|---|---|
| Liqueur coffee | 2.95 |
| Tea | 0.95 |

| Banana in coconut milk | 3.50 |
| Lychee in syrup with ice | 2.95 |
| Standard set meal | 12.50 |

**7** Save as **menu1**, print and save.

## Exercise 16

| *Skills* | ◯ Apply existing styles to a document |
| | ◯ Save existing document under another file format/ version number |

◯ Files required: **fashion.doc**

**1** Open the file **fashion.doc**.

**2** Change the orientation to landscape and the paper size to A4.

**3** Apply the *fashion* style to the heading and to the final paragraph.

**4** Select all of the text and apply 8 pt spacing above and below the paragraphs.

**5** Print the document.

**6** Save the file in web format.

**7** Close the file.

**3**

## Exercise 17

| *Skills* | ◯ Select word, line, sentence, paragraph, entire body text |
| | ◯ Use the **Undo/Redo** command |
| | ◯ Select number of copies to print |

◯ Files required: **race.doc**

**1** Open the file **race.doc**.

**2** Select the second paragraph and delete it.

**3**  Select the word **Olney** in the first paragraph and underline it.

**4**  Select all of the text and apply double-line spacing.

**5**  Select the first line of the final paragraph and embolden it.

**6**  Find and select the sentence: **At 11.30 a bell is rung to tell competitors to start frying pancakes.** Change this sentence to upper case.

**7**  Print two copies of the document.

**8**  Use the **Undo** command to change the sentence in step 6 back to its original case.

**9**  Change the entire document back to single-line spacing.

**10**  Change the display to landscape and set the left and right margins to 5 cm and the top and bottom margins to 4 cm.

**11**  Save the file as **race2**, print and close.

# Section 5 *Tables*

## Exercise 18

| Skills | ◯ Create a standard table |
| | ◯ Add borders |
| | ◯ Change cell attributes |

**1** Create a table showing the following.

| Mountain | Continent | Height (metres) |
|----------|-----------|-----------------|
| Everest | Asia | 8848 |
| Aconcagua | S. America | 6960 |
| McKinley | N. America | 6194 |
| Cook | Australasia | 3764 |

**2** Set the line width for all the borders in the table to 3 pt.

**3** Centre all the entries in column 3 (**Height** column).

**4** Save as **mountains.doc**.

**5** Print and close.

## Exercise 19

| Skills | ◯ Insert/delete columns/rows |
| | ◯ Remove borders |
| | ◯ Modify cell border width, style, colour |

Files required: **mountains.doc** (saved in Exercise 18)

**1** Open the file **mountains.doc** and resave as **mountains1**.

**2** Insert the following row after the **McKinley** row.

| Kilimanjaro | Africa | 5895 |
|-------------|--------|------|

3

**3** Insert a new column headed **Height (feet)** between the **Continent** and **Height (metres)** columns and enter the following heights in feet:

| Everest | 29029 |
|---|---|
| Aconcagua | 22834 |
| McKinley | 20320 |
| Kilimanjaro | 19340 |
| Cook | 12349 |

**4** Delete the **Aconcagua** row.

**5** Change the font in row 1 (the heading row) to Arial, 14 pt and embolden it.

**6** Change the column widths to display the data in row 1 on one row.

**7** Change the height of row 1 to 2 cm.

**8** Shade the background of the heading row to a colour other than white.

**9** Remove all the inside borders.

**10** Set the outside borders to **Double** line, 3 pt and colour Violet.

**11** Save as **mountains2**.

**12** Print one copy in landscape orientation and close.

# Section 6 *Mail Merge*

## Exercise 20

Skills  ○ Create a data file for use in a mail merge
       ○ Merge a data file with a letter document

Files required: **dirmeet.doc**

**1** Open the file **dirmeet.doc**.

**2** Spellcheck and save as **meet1** to be used as a merge letter.

**3** Create the following data source and save as **directors**:

| | | |
|---|---|---|
| Miss V Neck | Mrs A Other | Mr D Rom |
| 16 Pilgrims Way | 91 Gregory Gardens | 12 Tavistock Road |
| Kempston | Silsoe | Harrold |
| Bedford | Bedford | Bedford |
| MK32 9RH | BD27 6AQ | MK21 8JG |

**4** On the merge letter, replace the existing name and address with the merge fields:

<<Title>> <<Initial>> <<Last Name>>
<<Address1>>
<<Address2>>
<<Town>>
<<Postcode>>

**5** Merge the data source with the letter and save as **meetmerge**.

**6** Print the mail merged documents.

**7** Close all documents.

## Exercise 21

Skills  ○ Merge a data file with a label document

Files required: **directors.doc** (saved in Exercise 20)

**1** Use the data source created in Exercise 20 to create mailing labels.

**2** Print the labels on to A4 paper.

3

# Section 7 *Pictures, images and other objects*

## Exercise 22

> *Skills*  ◯ Insert a graphic into a document
> ◯ Resize a graphic

◉ Files required: **flower.doc**
**daisy.jpg**

1   Open the file **flower.doc**.

2   Insert the picture file **daisy.jpg** so that it is positioned above the text **Saturday 24 June**.

3   Resize the picture (keeping its original aspect ratio) so that it is approximately 3 cm square.

4   Centre the picture within the left and right margins.

5   Centre and format the text so that it looks attractive.

6   Add a border to the whole document.

7   Save as **flyer**, print and close.

8   Reopen **flyer.doc** and save in template format as **flyer.dot**.

9   Close the file.

## Exercise 23

> *Skills*  ◯ Move/duplicate a graphic within a document and between documents
> ◯ Delete a graphic
> ◯ Change display mode

◉ Files required: **deliver.doc**
**ideas.doc**

1   Open the file **deliver.doc**.

2   Change to **Print Layout View**.

**3** Change the header to read **Amended by (your name)**.

**4** Insert an automatic date in the Footer.

**5** Resave as **deliver1**.

**6** Copy the graphic on page 1 so that it also appears at the end of the document.

**7** Open the file **ideas.doc**.

**8** Cut the **hare** picture and paste it so that it is displayed after the following text in the **deliver1** file:

**If you mumble and rush, the audience will have a difficult job straining to understand.**

(*Note:* Start a new paragraph with the text **Alter the tone...**)

**9** Resave the **deliver1** file as **complete1**, print and close.

**10** In the **ideas** file, delete the **Twisted** graphic.

**11** Resave, print and close.

3

# Section 8 *Consolidation*

## Exercise 24

Files required: **brill rentals.doc**

1   Open the file **brill rentals.doc**.

2   Spellcheck and save the document as **brill2**.

3   Format the heading to Arial font, 16 pt and coloured green. Format to upper case.

4   Centre and embolden the line **PROBABLY THE BEST FOR MILES**.

5   Set the whole document to single-line spacing.

6   Amend the Footer text to read **Vehicle rentals 2006** and format to 10 pt and Arial font.

7   Insert page numbers at the top right, starting at 3.

8   Fully justify the first paragraph.

9   Indent the second paragraph at the left by 3 cm.

10   Insert a page break after the table.

11   Save as **brill3**, print and close.

## Exercise 25

Files required: **keyboard.doc**

1   Open the file **keyboard.doc**.

2   Create a new paragraph at the text beginning **If you have used a**… and at the text beginning **The keyboard has some extra keys**…

3   Add a header with an automatic filename and location and an automatic today's date.

4   Copy the first paragraph so that it appears at the end of the document.

5   Add a Shadow border to the new final paragraph. Set the border to 1 pt and shade the paragraph in grey.

**6** Change the line spacing of the first paragraph to double.

**7** Embolden the second paragraph.

**8** Select all the text in the document and apply 5 pt spacing between the paragraphs.

**9** Create a first-line indent of 2.25 cm for the first paragraph only.

**10** Save as **key2**, print the whole document in portrait display.

**11** On a separate sheet, print only the final paragraph in landscape display.

**12** Close the file.

## Exercise 26

*Note:* Answers to this exercise may vary so none is given.

**1** Open a new file and enter the following text:

This exercise will demonstrate my ability to do the following: use Help, display and hide toolbars, modify basic options/preferences and save a document in another file format such as:

Text file
Rich Text format
HTML
Template
Software-specific file extension
Version number

**2** Save as **abilities.doc** and print.

**3** Apply bullets to the list.

**4** Use the **Help** to search for information on **Word Count**.

**5** Copy and paste a few lines of this information to your current document.

**6** Start a new paragraph and explain how you display/hide toolbars.

**7** Start a new paragraph and state the procedure to modify the following options:

• User name
• Default folder to open/save documents.

**8** Start a new paragraph and explain briefly how to save a document in another file format (as listed above).

**9** Save the document as **abilities2**, print and close.

3

## Exercise 27

1   Open a new file and enter the following text:

Starter

Chicken soup Thai style cooked with chilli, herbs and lemon-sour, spicy and hot
Thai fish cakes fried in curry paste served with cucumber in sweet chilli sauce
Thai spring rolls stuffed with vegetables

Main Course

Chicken and cashew nuts Thai style
Beef cooked with chilli, peppers, carrots and mushrooms
Mixed seafood in Thai spicy sauce

Rice

Boiled Thai jasmine rice
Egg fried rice with chicken
Egg fried rice with prawns

2   Save as **menu.doc**.

3   Change the headings (**Starter, Main Course, Rice**) to 14 pt and an attractive font.

4   Insert a main heading **GOLDEN THAI RESTAURANT**. Format to 16 pt and to the same attractive font chosen in step 3.

5   Select all the text and centre between the margins.

6   Insert a suitable piece of clip art at the bottom of the menu and resize it to 4 cm wide.

7   Add the text **Golden Thai** © at the bottom left in 8 pt Arial.

8   Add a decorative border to the document.

9   Resave, print (set to A4 paper) and close.

## Exercise 28

1   Open a new file and create the following table:

| Anjelica Sidal | Marketing | Manager |
|---|---|---|
| Elyes Jhutti | Sales | Representative |
| Alicia Malone | Marketing | Administrator |
| Ralf Turner | Technical | Technician |

2   Insert a heading row at the top as follows:

   **Name          Department          Position**

3   Format the text in the heading row to bold.

4   Alter the heading row height to 1 cm.

5   Shade the heading cells.

6   Centre the text in the **Department** column (not the heading).

7   Set the outside table border to 3 pt and blue.

8   **Autofit to Contents** so that the text fits the cells.

9   Save as **staff** and print.

10   Delete the row entry for **Alicia**.

11   Reinsert the inside borders.

12   Insert a new column between the **Name** and **Department** columns, headed ☎ and enter the following numbers: **Anjelica 9081, Elyes 3452, Ralf 7655**.

13   Save as **staff update**, print and close.

**3**

## Exercise 29

Files required: **ven weather.doc**

**1** Open a new file and enter the following text (use tabs for the temperatures section):

Getting There:

By Air

Venice has one airport on the northern mainland of the lagoon. This is the Marco Polo Airport. There is also the Treviso Airport to the north. Direct flights can be booked from Europe and from New York. If you are travelling from Australia, Canada, New Zealand or other parts of the US, you will arrive at Rome or Milan and will have to make an onward journey to your destination.

Temperatures

| | | | |
|---|---|---|---|
| ▼ Jan | 6° | Cloud |
| ▼ Mar | 10° | Sun/showers |
| ▲ May | 20° | Sun/showers |
| ▼ Oct | 18° | Very wet |
| ▲ Dec | 7° | Sun/showers |

*Note:* ▼ Low season, ▲ High season

Venice has a varied climate and has well-defined seasons. The best months to go are May, June and September.

**2** Proofread and save as **venice.doc**.

**3** Open the file **ven weather.doc**, select the first paragraph and copy to the **venice** file so that it appears as part of the final paragraph after September.

**4** In the final paragraph, insert the following sentence after the sentence ending... **well-defined seasons**.

Humidity is high throughout the year.

**5** Format the first paragraph to have a first line indent of 1.50 cm and fully justify it.

**6** Automatically replace the word **extraordinary** with **exceptional**.

**7** Add **Venice** as a heading for the document. Format to a suitable font and change the size to 16 pt.

**8** Change the left and right margins to 1.5 cm.

**9** Switch to the file **ven weather** and move the chart from this document to the **venice.doc** file so that it appears above the final paragraph beginning **Venice has a varied climate**…

**10** Save the **venice** file as **Ven2** and print.

**11** Save the **ven weather** file as **weather2** and print.

**12** Close both files.

## Exercise 30

Files required: **keynesco.doc**
             **address directors.mdb**

**1** Open the file **keynesco.doc**.

**2** Insert today's date and the ref: **D129**.

**3** Below the ref, enter the following details:

**Present:**
**Mrs B Little (Chairman)**
**Mr D Light**
**Miss A Other**
**Mr L Vegas**

**4** Save as **minutes1** to be used as a merge letter.

**5** Use the file **address directors.mdb** as a data source to be merged with the **minutes1.doc**.

**6** In the merge letter, enter the merge fields where shown:

<<Title>> <<Last Name>>
<<Town>>

**7** Merge the data source with the letter and save as **minmerge**.

**8** Print the mailmerged documents.

**9** Close all documents.

3

# Spreadsheets

**Module 4**

## Section

1 Getting started

2 Editing

3 More formulae and functions

4 Formatting

5 Working with multiple worksheets/spreadsheet files

6 Charting

7 Consolidation

Please note that many skills are expanded upon and duplicated throughout the exercises.

**4**

# Section 1 *Getting started*

## Exercise 1

*Skills*
- Open/close a spreadsheet application
- Create a new spreadsheet
- Enter text and numeric data
- Enter simple formulae (addition)
- Save a spreadsheet
- Print a spreadsheet (showing data; showing formulae)
- Close a spreadsheet

**1** Load a spreadsheet application and create the following spreadsheet:

| | A | B | C | D |
|---|---|---|---|---|
| 1 | League | | | |
| 2 | Team | Won | Lost | Played |
| 3 | Giants | 10 | 5 | |
| 4 | Jets | 8 | 6 | |
| 5 | Eagles | 3 | 12 | |
| 6 | Lions | 12 | 4 | |

**2** Enter a simple formula in each of the cells D3, D4, D5 and D6 to calculate the number of games played for each team, i.e. **Won + Lost**.

**3** Check your spreadsheet for accuracy.

**4** Save the spreadsheet as **League(yr initials)**.

**5** Print one copy displaying the data and another displaying the formulae used.

**6** Close the spreadsheet file and exit the spreadsheet application.

# Exercise 2

*Skills*
- Enter simple formulae (multiplication, subtraction)
- Use Print Preview
- Print (fit to page)

1  Create the following spreadsheet and save as **Tour(yr initials)**:

| TOUR | | | | |
|------|------|-------|---------|--------|
| VENUE | COST | PRICE | NO SOLD | INCOME |
| YORK | 4000 | 30 | 900 | |
| LEEDS | 2700 | 20 | 769 | |
| BRISTOL | 6000 | 40 | 580 | |
| BATH | 5200 | 35 | 420 | |

2  In the **INCOME** column, enter formulae to calculate the income for each venue (**PRICE** multiplied by **NO SOLD**).

3  In the cell to the right of the heading **INCOME**, enter the heading **PROFIT**.

4  Enter formulae in the **PROFIT** column to calculate the profit for each venue (**INCOME** minus **COST**).

5  Save the spreadsheet as **Tour profit(yr initials)**.

6  Use print preview and print two copies showing values and one copy showing formulae. Ensure these fit on one page (use Fit to page).

7  Close the spreadsheet file.

4

## Exercise 3

*Skills*
- Use Sum or AutoSum
- Select cells
- Print (selection, select orientation, page size)

**1** Create the following spreadsheet (leave the cells containing 'formula' blank):

| Sales | | | | | | |
|---|---|---|---|---|---|---|
| Dept | Tue | Wed | Thu | Fri | Sat | Total |
| Food | 550 | 660 | 500 | 900 | 1120 | formula |
| Menswear | 200 | 190 | 300 | 100 | 780 | formula |
| Fashions | 300 | 625 | 740 | 800 | 1500 | formula |
| Baby | 200 | 450 | 380 | 590 | 213 | formula |
| Cosmetics | 77 | 90 | 65 | 105 | 280 | formula |
| Home | 500 | 1800 | 1200 | 954 | 3080 | formula |

**2** Save the spreadsheet as **store sales(yr initials)**.

**3** Enter a formula to calculate the **Total** for each department.

**4** Save the spreadsheet as **store sales2(yr initials)**.

**5** Print a copy of the spreadsheet in landscape orientation showing values.

**6** Print a copy in A4 size and in portrait orientation showing the formulae used. Use print preview and fit to one page.

**7** Select only the **Dept** and **Tue** columns and print. (Do not print cell **A1, Sales**.)

**8** Select only the **Dept**, **Food** and **Menswear** rows then print showing formulae (fit to one page).

**9** Close the spreadsheet.

# Section 2 *Editing*

## Exercise 4

| Skills | |
|---|---|
| | ○ Open an existing spreadsheet |
| | ○ Save a spreadsheet under another name and to a specified location |
| | ○ Use Zoom |
| | ○ Enter simple formulae (division) |
| | ○ Copy (replicate) formulae |
| | ○ Change margins |

Files required: **Seafood.xls**

4

**1** Open the spreadsheet file **Seafood.xls** and save as **Pasta(yr initials)** to your own work area.

**2** Zoom the display to 100%.

**3** In cell D6, use a simple formula to calculate the Linguine pasta Quantity for 1, i.e. divide cell C6 by 2.

**4** Copy this formula in the **Quantity for 1** column for all other ingredients.

**5** Save the file as **Pasta2(yr initials)**.

**6** Print one copy showing the formulae used, fit to one page on A4 paper, landscape orientation with the margins changed to left 3 cm and top 4 cm.

**7** Close the file.

## Exercise 5

*Skills*
- ◯ Amend cell entries
- ◯ Delete row/column
- ◯ Use Undo command
- ◯ Insert column
- ◯ Adjust formulae as necessary
- ◯ Print (display row/column headings, gridlines)
- ◯ Delete cell contents

Files required: **Store sales2(yr initials)** saved in Exercise 3

**1** Open the spreadsheet **store sales2(yr initials)** saved in Exercise 1.

**2** Change the following entries:
**Menswear Thu** should be 350 not 300
**Baby Fri** should be 610 not 590

**3** Delete the **Cosmetics** row.

**4** Delete the **Tue** column.

**5** Reinstate the **Tue** column using the **Undo** command.

**6** Delete the content of cell A1, i.e. **Sales**.

**7** Insert a new column headed **Mon** before the **Tue** column and enter the following data (adjust the spreadsheet formulae as necessary to include the sales for **Mon**):

| | |
|---|---|
| Food | 25 |
| Menswear | 180 |
| Fashions | 270 |
| Baby | 55 |
| Home | 25 |

**8** Save the spreadsheet as **store3(yr initials)**.

**9** Print one copy on A4 paper in landscape orientation, displaying gridlines and row and column headings.

**10** Close the spreadsheet.

## Exercise 6

*Skills*
- Insert row
- Use search, find and replace
- Use absolute cell reference
- Save in a different file format

Files required: **excursions.xls**

**1** Open the spreadsheet **excursions.xls** and save in your own work area as **trips(yr initials)**.

**2** Insert a new row between (rows 9 and 10) **YORK** and **POOLE** with the following details:

**LONDON, TRIP CODE =44Z, COST GBP= 30.00, MEALS=15**

**3** Use the find and replace command to automatically replace all **BRISTOL** entries with **BURFORD**.

**4** Use the search command to find the entry **1YY** and key in **16Y**.

**5** Change the entries as follows: in A15 to read **Group B** and in A29 to read **Group D**.

**6** In cell D7, enter a formula to calculate the cost in euros. Use the conversion rate in cell B3 and make this reference absolute, i.e. cost in GBP multiplied by conversion rate.

**7** Copy the formula in cell D7 for Burford and York in Group A.

**8** Save the amended spreadsheet as **euro costed trips(yr initials)**.

**9** Print the spreadsheet in landscape displaying formulae used, showing gridlines and fitting to one page.

**10** Save the spreadsheet as a template named **trips 2005.xlt**.

**11** Close the spreadsheet files.

4

# Section 3 *More formulae and functions*

## Exercise 7

| Skills | Use functions: Min, Max |
|---|---|

Files required: **League(yr initials)** saved in Exercise 1

1 Open the spreadsheet **League(yr initials)**.

2 On a new row, add the team **Bears**, who to date have won 10 and lost 6.

3 Copy the formula from cell D6 to D7 to give a total played for the **Bears** (this may be done automatically).

4 The **Giants** have now won 11; amend this entry and ensure that the **Played** figure is still correct.

5 In cell A9, enter the text **Top** and, in cell B9, use the **Max** function to generate the highest number of games won.

6 In cell A10, enter the text **Bottom** and, in cell B10, use the **Min** function to generate the lowest number of games won.

7 Save as **League2(yr initials)** and print the amended spreadsheet showing formulae.

8 Close the spreadsheet file.

## Exercise 8

| Skills | Use logical If function |
|---|---|
| | Use functions: Average, Count |
| | Apply automatic title row printing |

Files required: **aj clothing.xls**

1 Open the spreadsheet **aj clothing.xls** and save in your own work area as **clothing(yr initials)**.

2 Print the spreadsheet in landscape with row 5 (the heading row) repeated automatically on the second page.

3   Move to cell B27 and use the **Count** function to count the number of clothing items for men.

4   Move to cell B44 and use the **Count** function to count the number of clothing items for women.

5   Move to cell B65 and use the **Count** function to count the number of household items.

6   Move to cell A67 and enter the text **Av. No**.

7   In cell B67, use the **Average** function to generate the average number of items in the three sections (i.e. the average of B27, B44 and B65).

8   In cell G6, enter a formula to display **Yes** if the **Reorder level** figure is greater than the **No in stock** figure and **No** if the reorder figure is less than the **No in stock** figure.

9   Replicate this formula through cells G7 to G26.

10  Save as **clothing2(yr initials)** and print the amended spreadsheet displaying the formula used, column and row headings and fitting to one page.

11  Make another print showing only cells E5 to G26, showing data, without column and row headings.

12  Close the spreadsheet file.

4

## Exercise 9

Files required: **Cities.xls**

1   Open the spreadsheet **Cities.xls** and save in your own work area as **cities(yr initials)**.

2   In cell F3, enter the text **Average**.

3   In cell F4, enter a formula to generate the average temperature in **Amsterdam** over the four month period.

4   Copy this formula in this column to generate the average temperatures in the other cities.

5   In cell G3, enter the text **Suitability**.

6   Move to cell G4 and enter a formula to display **Too hot** if the Average temperature is above 25° C and **OK** otherwise.

7   Replicate this formula for the other cities.

**8**  Move to cell A20 and enter the text **Maximum**.

**9**  In cell B20, enter a formula to generate the maximum May temperature.

**10**  Move to cell A21 and enter the text **Minimum**.

**11**  In cell B21, enter a formula to generate the minimum May temperature.

**12**  Save the spreadsheet as **cities OK(yr initials)** and print one copy showing the data.

**13**  Close the spreadsheet file.

# Section 4 *Formatting*

## Exercise 10

*Skills*
- Embolden, centre cell entries
- Widen columns
- Display numeric data to two decimal places
- Display commas in numeric values
- Display monetary values
- Centre a title across a cell range
- Change font size, type

Files required: **store3(yr initials)** saved in Exercise 5

1 Open the spreadsheet **store3(yr initials)**.

2 Embolden and centre the column headings, i.e. A2 to H2.

3 In cell A1, insert the heading **Sales** with a size 16 pt and Wide Latin type.

4 Centre the main heading **Sales** across columns A–H.

5 Display all the numeric data to two decimal places with commas to denote thousands.

6 Enter a new row headed **Average Store Sales** (in cell A8). Widen the column to display the new entry in full.

7 In this row, enter a formula (in cell B8) to calculate the average daily sales for **Mon**.

8 Replicate the formula for the other days and format the average daily sales figures to display a £ sign.

9 Change the row heading **Fashions** to **Ladies' Fashions**.

10 Save the spreadsheet as **store format4(yr initials)** and print one copy in landscape display showing the data. Do not show row and column headings.

11 Close the spreadsheet file.

4

## Exercise 11

*Skills*
- Change column to a specified width
- Change row to a specified height
- Wrap cell content
- Insert/amend headers/footers
- Display numbers as integers
- Italicise cell entries
- Shade cells

Files required: **electrical.xls**

1  Open the spreadsheet **electrical.xls** and save to your own work area as **electrical(yr initials)**.

2  Change the width of column D to 20.

3  Change the width of column H to 11 and, in cell H1, enter the heading **Extended guarantee** and wrap this heading so that it displays in full in its own cell.

4  Change the height of row 1 to 45.

5  In the header, left section, add an automatic entry displaying today's date.

6  In the footer, change the entry to read **Amended by (insert your name)**.

7  Change the numeric entries in column G to display as integers.

8  In cells A2 to A7, italicise the entries and change the text colour to green.

9  Change the shading in row 1 to blue.

10  Save the spreadsheet as **electrical goods(yr initials)** and print one copy in landscape orientation displaying row and column headings.

11  Close the spreadsheet file.

## Exercise 12

*Skills*
- Add/remove borders
- Adjust row height
- Adjust cell content orientation
- Underline/double underline cell entries
- Use the format painter
- Format date
- Add currency symbols
- Format cells to display percentages

Files required: **aj clothing.xls**

**1** Open the file **aj clothing.xls** and save in your own work area as **shopping(yr initials)**.

**2** In cell B2, change the date format to display the date in full, i.e. 12 August 2005.

**3** In cell E5 (**No in stock**), set the orientation to 90 degrees.

**4** In row 5, adjust the height to 60.

**5** Format all entries in the **Code** column to display to three decimal places.

**6** Display all entries in the **Price** column to display with a £ sign to two decimal places.

**7** Remove the border in cell A2.

**8** Place a Thick Box Border around the section A4 to G26, i.e. Men's clothing section.

**9** Double underline the entry in cell A4 and add blue shading to this cell.

**10** Use the format painter to copy this format to cells A29 and A45.

**11** In cell D2, enter the number 0.01 and format to display as percentage.

**12** Save the spreadsheet as **shopping2(yr initials)** and print one copy fitting to one page.

**13** Close the spreadsheet file.

4

# Section 5 *Working with multiple worksheets/spreadsheet files*

## Exercise 13

> *Skills* ○ Work with worksheets (insert new, delete, duplicate)
> ○ Sort data into ascending/descending numerical order
> ○ Use cut/copy and paste to move/duplicate cell contents to another part of the spreadsheet

Files required: **Getaway breaks.xls**

1 Open the spreadsheet file **Getaway breaks.xls** and save it to your own work area with the name **breaks(yr initials)**.

2 Insert a new worksheet with the name **Forest**.

3 Copy cells A25 to D28 from the **Properties** worksheet to the **Forest** worksheet.

4 On the **Properties** worksheet, sort the **Country** properties into ascending numerical order of **Booked(A)**.

5 Duplicate the worksheet **Per location** and name the new sheet **No of locations**.

6 On the properties worksheet, move the **Bookings** section (cells H4 to J13) to the bottom of this sheet starting at row 74.

7 Delete the worksheet **Country column chart**.

8 Save the file as **getaway(yr initials)**.

9 Print all sheets in the workbook, fitting each sheet to one page.

10 Close the spreadsheet file.

## Exercise 14

Skills
⬡ Open several spreadsheet files
⬡ Move cell contents between active spreadsheets
⬡ Use Autofill to increment entries
⬡ Work with worksheets (rename)

Files required: **Ross.xls**
**hampers.xls**

1  Open the file **hampers.xls** and save to your own work area as **hampers(yr initials)**.

2  Rename the worksheet **money flow**.

3  Open the file **Ross.xls** and save to your own work area as **Ross(your initials)**.

4  Rename the **March** worksheet **April**.

5  Return to the **hampers(yr initials)** spreadsheet file and copy the content of cell A35 to cell A26 on the **April** worksheet of the **Ross(yr initials)** spreadsheet.

6  On the **money flow** worksheet of the **hampers(yr initials)** file, Autofill the date entries down to cell A31.

7  On the **money flow** worksheet, format all date entries to dd.m.yy, e.g. 10.1.05.

8  On the **money flow** worksheet, format all data in columns B and C to with two decimal places.

9  Resave both files.

10  Print both spreadsheets.

11  Close the spreadsheet files.

**4**

## Exercise 15

Files required: **students.xls**

1   Open the spreadsheet **students.xls** and save it to your work area with the
name **students(yr initials)**.

2   Sort the data in cells B14 to B20 into ascending alphabetical order
(remember to show associated data).

3   Freeze the column titles in row 7.

4   Scroll down the spreadsheet and sort the data in cells B42 to B46 into
descending alphabetical order.

5   Unfreeze the column titles in row 7.

6   Save the spreadsheet as **courses(yr initials)**.

7   Print one copy fitting to page.

8   Close the spreadsheet file.

# Section 6  *Charting*

## Exercise 16

| Skills | |
| --- | --- |
| ◌ | Produce column chart |
| ◌ | Add/amend titles and labels |
| ◌ | Change chart type |
| ◌ | Print chart |

Files required: **distances.xls**

1   Open the spreadsheet **distances.xls** and save it to your work area with the name **distances(yr initials)**.

2   Create a column chart comparing the distances from **Bristol** to **Brighton**, **Edinburgh** and **Cardiff** as follows (use cells B6 to D6 and B9 to D9):

- chart title: **Distances from Bristol**
- label the x axis **Destination**
- label the y axis **Distance in miles**
- save the chart on a new sheet and name the sheet **Bristol**
- change the scale to display to 500
- do not include a legend.

3   Save the spreadsheet file as **chart1(yr initials)**.

4   Print the chart in landscape orientation.

5   Change the chart to a clustered column with 3-D visual effect.

6   Amend the chart title to **Road Travel: Bristol**.

7   Change the destination names on the x axis to 16 pt.

8   Save the file as **chart2(yr initials)**.

9   Print a copy of the chart.

10   Close the spreadsheet file.

**4**

## Exercise 17

> *Skills*  ○ Produce comparative bar chart/line graph
> ○ Resize, move chart

Files required: **Tax.xls**

**1**  Open the spreadsheet **Tax.xls** and save it to your work area with the name **Tax(yr initials)**.

**2**  Create a comparative bar chart comparing the tax band A and tax band F for all areas as follows:

- chart title **Bands A and F**
- label the x axis **Area**
- label the y axis **Cost (£)**
- save the chart on the same sheet as the original data (ensure data is not obscured)
- include a legend
- ensure all bars for Band A are green.

**3**  Save the spreadsheet file as **tax charts(yr initials)**.

**4**  Print a copy of the chart only.

**5**  Change the chart type to a *line with markers displayed at each data value*.

**6**  Change the chart background colour to yellow.

**7**  Save the spreadsheet file as **tax charts2(yr initials)**.

**8**  Print a copy of the spreadsheet data and chart on the same page.

**9**  Close the spreadsheet file.

# Exercise 18

1   Create the following spreadsheet and save as **fruit(yr initials)**:

| Fruit Preferences | Sample of 250 |
|---|---|
| Apple | 47 |
| Banana | 72 |
| Orange | 60 |
| Pineapple | 51 |
| Undecided | 20 |

2   Create an *exploded pie* chart showing the fruit preferences (including those undecided) as follows:

  • chart title **Fruit Preferences (sample of 250)**
  • include a legend
  • show percentages for each of the segments
  • save the chart on its own sheet named **Fruit pie**.

3   Pull out the segment for **Banana** to emphasise the favourite.

4   Save the spreadsheet file as **Fruit favourite(yr initials)**.

5   Delete the legend and instead add data labels to the segments.

6   Duplicate the pie chart to another sheet named **Pie2**.

7   Save the spreadsheet file as **Fruit pie2(yr initials)**.

8   Print only the **Pie2** sheet, fitted to one page.

9   Close the spreadsheet file.

4

# Section 7 *Consolidation*

## Exercise 19

*Note:* This is a theory exercise.

Open a word-processing application and answer the following questions.

**1**  Explain how you would access help in Excel.

**2**  In Excel help, search for help on the **Undo** and **Redo** commands. Read the results of the search and then copy and paste the result into your work document. (Do not worry if any graphics are not displayed.)

**3**  Why is it important to check spreadsheets for accuracy before distributing them?

**4**  Which menu and options would you use to modify basic options in Excel, such as user name, and default folder to open/save documents?

**5**  What do the following error messages mean?
   - ####
   - #REF
   - #VALUE
   - #DIV/0!
   - #NUM
   - #NAME

**6**  Explain the following terms: relative cell referencing; absolute cell referencing; mixed cell referencing.

## Exercise 20

Files required: **media.xls**

**1**  Open the file **media.xls** and save the file to your own work area as **media(yr initials)**.

**2**  On the **CD Sales** worksheet, zoom the display to 100%.

**3**  Widen column A to display the entries in full.

**4**  Duplicate the **CD Sales** sheet and rename the duplicate **CD Sales2**.

**5**  On the **CD Sales** worksheet, insert the figure **345** in cell B8 and **212** in D10.

**6** Amend the figure in cell D7 to **375**.

**7** In cell A11, enter the text **TOTAL**. Embolden and italicise it.

**8** In cell B11, enter formula to total the sales for the month of Jan.

**9** Replicate the formula to the cells C11 and D11.

**10** Double-underline cells A11, B11, C11, D11.

**11** Display the values in the **TOTAL** row to two decimal places with a £ sign.

**12** Delete the worksheet **Games** and rename the worksheet **Movie Sales** to **DVD Sales**.

**13** On sheet **DVD Jan**, change the chart as follows:

- chart type to **Column**
- delete the legend
- change the chart background colour to green and the columns to red
- on the y axis change the data range to max 650.

**14** Move the chart so that it appears on sheet **DVD Sales**. Resize it so that it does not obscure data.

**15** Delete the **DVD Jan** sheet.

**16** Save the file as **media2**.

**17** Print the worksheets **CD Sales** and **DVD Sales** displaying only row/column headings and gridlines.

**18** Close the file.

## Exercise 21

Files required: **accounts.xls**

**1** Open the file **accounts.xls** and save to your work area as **AccountsJan**.

**2** Widen column D to 30.

**3** Change the height of row 3 to display the data in full.

**4** In cell E11, enter a formula that subtracts cell C26 from cell E7.

**5** Enter a formula in cell E12 that displays the text **Credit** if the amount in cell E11 is greater than zero and **Debit** if it is less then zero.

**6** Format all monetary amounts to display a € sign, comma and two decimal places.

7  Centre the text in cell A1 across the cells A1 to E1. Change the font to Century and 14 pt.

8  Shade cells A4 and A17 in green.

9  Insert a header with an automatic today's date.

10  Amend the footer to read **Amended by** *your name*.

11  Change the margins to 4 cm top and 4 cm bottom.

12  Save the file as **accounts(yr initials)**.

13  Print two copies in landscape display, one showing data and the other showing formulae. Use Print Preview and fit to page where necessary.

14  Close the file.

## Exercise 22

1  Create the following spreadsheet file and save as **marks(your initials)** with the attributes below:
   - format the date as DD/MM/YYYY
   - centre the cells containing **Test 1**, **Test 2** and **Test 3**.

| | A | B | C | D |
|---|---|---|---|---|
| 1 | Marks | | | |
| 2 | Today's date | | | |
| 3 | | Jane | Jim | Jack |
| 4 | Test 1 | 13 | 27 | 23 |
| 5 | Test 2 | 16 | 29 | 32 |
| 6 | Test 3 | 19 | 31 | 34 |

2  In cell E3, enter the text **Average Test Mark** and wrap this cell content.

3  In cell E4, using the **Average** function, enter a formula to calculate the average mark for **Test 1**. Replicate for **Test 2** and **Test 3**.

4  Format the numbers in column E to integer.

5  Delete the column for **Jim**.

6  Insert a new column before the **Jane** column with data as below. Adjust formulae as necessary.

   **Jill, Test 1: 30, Test 2: 32, Test 3: 29**

7  Create a comparative bar chart on the same sheet (accept default bar chart) from the data in cells A3 to D6.

8  In cell A7, enter the text **Total**.

9  In cell B7, enter a formula to add the test marks for **Jill**. Replicate for the other candidates.

10 Insert a new row below row 1. In cell A2, enter the text **Pass mark**. In cell B2, enter the number **50**.

11 In cell B9, enter a formula that displays **Pass** if the number is greater than the number in cell B2 (make this cell reference absolute) and otherwise displays **Fail**. Replicate to C9 and D9.

12 Save the spreadsheet as **Test2(yr initials)** and print one copy showing all the data.

13 Print a further copy showing only the chart.

14 Close the file.

## Exercise 23

Files required: **shoes.xls**

1  Open the spreadsheet file **shoes.xls** and resave it to your work area as **shoes(yr initials)**.

2  Delete the entry in cell I3.

3  In cell C3, set the orientation to 90 degrees.

4  Copy the formatting of cell A3 to cells A28, A29 and A30. Adjust cell widths as necessary.

5  Use search and replace to change all entries for **Moccasins** to **Slippers**.

6  Sort the items from row 4 to row 26 in ascending **Retail Price** order and then in alphabetical **Colour** order.

7  In cell H4, enter a formula to calculate the profit per item (**Retail Price** minus **Cost Price**). Replicate this formula for all items.

8  In cell G4, enter a formula to calculate the total profit (**Profit per item** multiplied by **No Sold**). Replicate this formula for all items.

9  In cell B28, use the **Count** function to display the number of different items in stock.

4

**10** Change the entries in cells A29 and A30 to read **Minimum Cost Price** and **Maximum Cost Price** respectively.

**11** In cell B29, create a formula that calculates the minimum cost price for an individual item.

**12** In cell B30, create a formula that calculates the maximum cost price for an individual item.

**13** Delete row 2.

**14** In cell A1, insert the text **Everyday Shoes** and centre it across the columns A to H.

**15** Add a Thick Box Border to the cells A1 to H29.

**16** Remove the border from the cell in column A containing the text **ANALYSIS**.

**17** Save the file as **shoes2(yr initials)**.

**18** Print one copy in portrait display and fitting to one page.

**19** Print a copy displaying formulae of column B only.

**20** Save another copy of the file as **shoes2(yr initials).rtf** (Rich Text Format).

**21** Close the files.

## Exercise 24

Files required: **survey.xls**

**1** Open the spreadsheet file **survey.xls** and save in your own work area as **survey(yr initials)**.

**2** Autofill the entries in cells A9 to A13.

**3** In cell B18, enter a formula to calculate the number of visits per year (B14 multiplied by 52).

**4** In cell B19, enter a formula to calculate the number of visits per month (B18 divided by 12).

**5** Format cells C22, C23 and C24 to display percentages.

**6** Save as **survey amended** and print in landscape orientation.

**7** Duplicate the spreadsheet content to a new spreadsheet file. Save the new file as **results**.

**8** Switch back to the **survey amended** spreadsheet file and insert a new sheet with the name **No polled Oct**.

**9** Open the spreadsheet file **Jan poll Numbers** and Autofill the date entries in column A so that they go to the end of November.

**10** Freeze row 4 and scroll though the spreadsheet deleting any dates when **No Polled** displays zero in column B.

**11** Unfreeze row 4.

**12** Copy cells A4 through to B21 from the **Jan poll number** file to the **survey amended** file, sheet **No polled Oct**.

**13** On the **Jan poll numbers** file, insert a header that automatically displays the worksheet name **No polled**.

**14** Resave all files with their original names.

**15** Print the **Jan poll numbers** file only, set the top and bottom margins to 8 cm and automatically display row 4 at the top of page 2.

**16** Close all files.

4

# Database

## Section

Please note that many skills are expanded upon and duplicated throughout the exercises.

5

# Section 1 *Getting started*

### Exercise 1

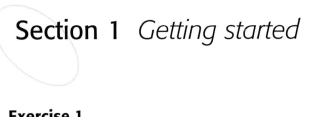

**1** Start up Access.

**2** Set up the following database **Speed Cycles** with field types and properties as shown below. Do not set a primary key.

**3** Save the table as **Staff**.

| Field Name | Data Type | Field Size or Format |
|---|---|---|
| Staff ID | Text | 4 |
| Surname | Text | 20 |
| First Name | Text | 20 |
| Hourly Pay (£) | Currency | Fixed |

**4** Enter the following data:

| Staff ID | Surname | First Name | Hourly Pay (£) |
|---|---|---|---|
| S345 | Merriman | Rob | 6.50 |
| S231 | Young | Malcolm | 6.25 |
| S789 | Ramm | James | 6.00 |
| D452 | Kew | Daisy | 5.75 |
| D129 | Schaal | Joe | 6.00 |

**5** Close the file.

## Exercise 2

*Skills*
- Define a primary key
- Change column width
- Modify field attributes

1 Set up the following database called **cooktime** with field types and properties as shown below. Set the **Recipe Code** field as the primary key. In the **Type** field, add a description **S=Starter, M=Main, D=Dessert**. Save the table as **Recipes**.

| Field Name | Data Type | Field Size or Format |
|---|---|---|
| Recipe Code | AutoNumber | Long Integer |
| Name | Text | 40 |
| Type | Text | 1 |
| Prep time (mins) | Number | Long Integer |
| Cook time (mins) | Number | Long Integer |
| Cals | Number | Long Integer |

2 Enter the data below. (In the **Type** field use the codes as follows: **S:Starter, M:Main, D:Dessert**.)

| Recipe Code | Name | Type | Prep time (mins) | Cook time (mins) | Cals |
|---|---|---|---|---|---|
| AutoNumber | Mango Fool | Dessert | 20 | 0 | 475 |
| | Maple-glazed Turkey | Main | 10 | 25 | 290 |
| | Crispy Prawns | Starter | 10 | 6 | 209 |
| | Spicy Chicken Provencale | Main | 10 | 40 | 230 |
| | Smoked Cod and Spinach Bake | Main | 10 | 30 | 165 |

3 Widen the columns in the table to display the data entries in full.

4 Close the file.

# Section 2 *Editing*

## Exercise 3

| Skills | |
|---|---|
| *Skills* | ◯ Open an existing database |
| | ◯ Print data in table format |
| | ◯ Navigate through a table |
| | ◯ Modify data |
| | ◯ Add a primary key and index |
| | ◯ Set print orientation, page size |

Files required: **Speed Cycles** (saved in Exercise 1)

1 Open the database **Speed Cycles** saved in Exercise 1.

2 Open the table **Staff** and print all the records in table format.

3 Make the following amendments:

 • the **Staff ID** for **Malcolm Young** should read **D231** not **S231**
 • the **Hourly Pay** for **Daisy Kew** should be **6.75** not **5.75**
 • **Rob Merriman**'s surname has incorrect spelling – amend to **Meriman**.

4 Preview then print all records in table format in landscape orientation, setting the paper to size **Letter**.

5 Change to table design view and set the **Staff ID** field as the primary key and index with no duplicates.

6 Save the table and close the file.

## Exercise 4

*Skills*
- Add a new field
- Delete data
- Delete a field
- Change field order
- Insert records
- Set validation rules and validation text

Files required: **cooktime** (saved in Exercise 2)

1  Open the database file **cooktime** saved in Exercise 2.

2  Open the table **Recipes** and print all records in table format and landscape orientation.

3  Switch to table design view and enter a new **Yes/No** field with the name **Freezable**.

4  Set the following recipes to **Yes** in the new **Freezable** field:
- Spicy Chicken Provencale
- Smoked Cod and Spinach Bake
- Maple-glazed Turkey.

5  Amend the records as follows:
- **Crispy Prawns** to read **Crispy King Prawns**
- **Mango Fool** should be **400 cals**.

6  Change the name of the **Cals** field to **Cals (per portion)**. Set a validation rule in this field **<450** and the validation text to **Must be less than 450 cals**. Widen this field column so that the field name is displayed in full.

7  Delete the **Type** field.

8  Change the field order so that the **Cals (per portion)** field comes before the **Prep time (mins)** field.

**9**   Insert the following new records:

| Recipe Code | Name | Cals (per portion) | Prep time (mins) | Cook time (mins) | Freezable |
|---|---|---|---|---|---|
| Auto Number | Baked Spiced Plums with Ricotta | 110 | 5 | 20 | No |
| | Thai Mackerel parcels | 325 | 15 | 20 | Yes |
| | Mulled Pears in Cider | 85 | 10 | 30 | No |

**10**   Print all the records in table format in landscape orientation.

**11**   Close the file.

## Exercise 5

| *Skills* | ◯ Delete records |
|---|---|

Files required: **Speed Cycles** (saved in Exercise 3)

**1**   Open the database **Speed Cycles** saved in Exercise 3.

**2**   Open the table **Staff** and delete the record for Staff ID **D129**.

**3**   Add a new field **Start Date** after **Staff ID** with the following properties:
Data Type: Date/Time, Format: Medium Date.

**4**   Add the data to this field as follows:

| Surname | Start Date |
|---|---|
| Meriman | 21/2/05 |
| Young | 27/6/05 |
| Ramm | 24/10/05 |
| Kew | 15/5/06 |

**5** Add the following records:

| Staff ID | Start Date | Surname | First name | Hourly Pay (£) |
|----------|-----------|---------|-----------|----------------|
| N781 | 21/8/06 | Bouzova | Skye | 5.50 |
| N218 | 24/7/06 | Jones | Dylan | 5.30 |
| D411 | 4/9/06 | Jonson | Olisa | 6.00 |

**6** Print all records in portrait orientation.

**7** Close the file.

## Exercise 6

Files required: **Surgery**

**1** Open the database **Surgery** and the table **Animals**.

**2** Amend the table design as follows:
- set the **TIME** field to Medium Time
- add a description to the **TYPE** field as follows:
  **B=Bird, C=Cat, D=Dog, O=Other**
- set the **REF NO** field size to 3
- in the day field set a validation rule **Not Mon** and validation text **Surgery is closed on Mondays**
- set the **REF NO** field as the primary key.

**3** Delete the following records:
- ref no **K57, Hamster**
- ref no **P99, Rabbit**.

**4** Add the following record:

| Type | Breed | Ref No | Day | Time | Previous Visits |
|------|-------|--------|-----|------|-----------------|
| D | Spaniel | L99 | Tue | 12.30 | 0 |

**5** Amend the following records:
- the **Goose**, ref. no. P21 appointment is now 18.00
- the **Beagle**, ref. no. J90 has had 6 previous visits.

**6** Print all records in table format, landscape orientation, and set to A4.

**7** Close the file.

5

### Exercise 7

Files required: **woollens**

1 Open the database **woollens** and the table **STOCK**.

2 Working with the table **STOCK**, amend the table design as follows:
  • set the **CODE** field to be the primary key indexed with no duplicates
  • set the **PRICE** Data Type to Currency so that a £ symbol will be displayed
  • delete the **FABRIC** field
  • move the **CODE** field so that it is the first field.

3 Widen the **DESIGN** field so that its contents are displayed in full.

4 Print the **STOCK** table in landscape and close this table.

5 Open the **FEB** table and delete all records with the colour **APRICOT**.

6 Print the **FEB** table in landscape and close.

7 Close the file.

# Section 3  *Sorting and searching*

## Exercise 8

*Skills:*      ○ Add/remove filters
               ○ Set print range
               ○ Find a record on given criteria

Files required: **rentals**

1  Open the **rentals** database and the **Props** table.

2  Use the **Sort** button to sort the table into ascending alphabetical order of **Property Name**.

3  Print the sorted table in landscape orientation.

4  Print only the records with **Property Name** beginning with the letters A, B and C.

5  Use the **Find** button to search for all records with 3 bedrooms. Note down the names of the properties.

6  Use a filter to find all properties with a change date of **Friday** and that allow pets.

7  Print the results of step 6 in landscape orientation.

8  Remove the filtering.

9  Close the file.

5

## Exercise 9

*Skills*
- ◯ Create a simple query
- ◯ Create a query with multiple criteria
- ◯ Save a query
- ◯ Add/remove/hide/unhide fields in a query
- ◯ Select and sort records based on given criteria
- ◯ Select and sort records using logical operators
- ◯ Delete a query
- ◯ Search for a specific word

Files required: **rentals** (saved in Exercise 8)

1 Open the **rentals** database, saved in Exercise 8, and the **Props3** table.

2 Search for Property name **Cliffs** and change to **Hilltop**.

3 Create a query based on the **Props3** table to search for all properties with **Maggie** as the agent. Save as **Maggie**.

4 Print details of the selected records in landscape orientation showing all fields.

5 Create a query based on the **Props3** table to search for all properties with less than 4 bedrooms that allow pets. Save as **less than 4bed+pets**.

6 Sort the results in descending order of **Price Code**. Print the query results, in portrait orientation, with only the fields **Property Name** and **Price Code**.

7 Close the query.

8 Open the query **3beds>4** and print in portrait orientation.

9 Change the criteria of the query **3beds>4** to show all properties with more than 6 occupants. Save the amended query as **3beds>6** and print.

10 Delete the query **With TV**.

11 Open the query **all props**:
   - unhide the **Change Day** field
   - delete the **Pets** field
   - hide the **Price Code** field
   - resave the query and print the result.

12 Close the file.

# Exercise 10

*Skills*  ◯  **Move fields in a query**

Files required: **woollens2**

**1** Open the database **woollens2**.

**2** Open the query **Less than £20** and change the criteria in the **Price** field to less than or equal to 30.

**3** Sort the query into alphabetical order of **Colour** and save as **less than £30**.

**4** Print the query displaying **Colour**, **Fabric** and **Price** fields only.

**5** Create a new query (save as **Purple**) using the table **STOCK2** to search for all purple sweaters in the price range between £30 and £40 (inclusive). Change the field order so that **CODE** in the first field displayed.

**6** Print the query result.

**7** Create a new query (save as **cashmere**) using the **STOCK2** table to find all **cashmere** jumpers that are not of neck type Polo (**PO**) or Round (**RD**).

**8** Sort the query result into descending order of price and print all fields and all records in landscape orientation.

**9** Close the file.

5

# Section 4 *Reporting*

## Exercise 11

| Skills | |
|---|---|
| | ○ Create reports |
| | ○ Present selected data in a particular sequence on screen and in reports |
| | ○ Modify a report |
| | ○ Create and customise footers |
| | ○ Group data in a report |

Files required: **house**

1   Open the database **house**.

2   Produce a report based on the **Properties** table as follows:
   a Display all fields except **Date Registered** and all the records.
   b Group by **Office**.
   c Sort in ascending order of **Price**.
   d Title the report **Properties grouped by office**.
   e Add a footer with the text **Report produced by (your name)** and the current time of day in Arial, bold, 12 pt.

3   Print the report.

4   Change report title to **Properties for Sale, grouped by office (insert today's date)**.

5   Save and print the report.

6   Close the file.

## Exercise 12

*Skills*  ◯ Group data in a report – totals, subtotals etc.
◯ Create and customise headers

Files required: **house**

1  Open the database **house**.

2  Produce a report based on the **Properties** table as follows:
   • include all fields except **Date Registered** and **Property Ref**
   • group the report by **Office**
   • add totals and sub-totals for the field **Price**
   • sort the report into descending order of **Price**
   • add a title **Properties prices totalled**
   • add a header with your name.

3  Save and print the report.

4  Open the report **Properties prices totalled**.

5  Add the date to the header and resave the report.

6  Print page 1 only.

7  Close the file.

**5**

## Exercise 13

Files required: **names**

1  Open the database **names**.

2  Produce a report based on the query **Birmingham or Milton Keynes**.

   • Include all fields included in the query.
   • Sort into descending order of **LAST NAME**.
   • Add a title **Midlands**.
   • Add a footer with **Produced by (yr name) from query**.

3  Save and print the report.

4  Delete the report **Labels people**.

5  Close the file.

# Section 5 *Forms*

## Exercise 14

| Skills | |
|---|---|
| | ○ Create a simple form |
| | ○ Enter data |
| | ○ Format text |
| | ○ Change background |
| | ○ Apply filter, remove filter |

Files required: **cooktime** (saved in Exercise 4)

1   Open the database **cooktime** saved in Exercise 4.

2   Create a simple form using the table **Recipes**.

3   Change the text of the **Field** headings to Times New Roman, italic, 10 pt.

4   Change the colour of the background in the **Field** headings boxes to yellow.

5   Add a header displaying your name.

6   Enter the following new records:

| Recipe Code | Name | Cals (per portion) | Prep time (mins) | Cook time (mins) | Freezable |
|---|---|---|---|---|---|
| AutoNumber | Banana and Ginger Cake | 140 | 15 | 50 | Yes |
| | Red Pepper and Orange Soup | 35 | 10 | 15 | No |

7   Delete the record for **Mulled Pears in Cider**.

8   Amend the record **Smoked Cod and Spinach Bake** to read **Smoked Cod and Broccoli Bake**.

9   Print pages one and two in Form format.

10   Apply a filter and find all the recipes that are freezable. Write down the number then remove the filter.

**11**  Save the form as **dishes**.

**12**  Close the file.

## Exercise 15

*Skills*  ◯  **Change arrangement of objects within a form layout**

Files required: **vet**

**1**  Open the database **vet** and the form **appointments**.

**2**  Change the text of the data to a different font type, bold, 8 pt.

**3**  Change the colour of the background of the data boxes to blue.

**4**  Move the **Time** field so that it is displayed above the **Day** field.

**5**  Enter the following new record:

| Type | Breed | Ref no | Day | Time | Previous visits |
|------|-------|--------|-----|------|-----------------|
| O | SNAKE | K90 | THU | 16:00 | 3 |

**6**  Save the database and print the new record only in Form format.

**7**  Close the file.

5

# Section 6 *Working with more than one table*

## Exercise 16

Skills
- Relate tables in a database
- Create relationships between tables
- Set relationship rules between tables
- Delete database objects

Files required: **office store**

1   Open the database **office store**.

2   Create a one-to-one relationship between the **Customer ID** field of the **Contact details** table and the **Customer ID** field of the **Bank** table. Apply referential integrity to the relationship.

3   Create a query using the tables **Contact details** and **bank** as follows:

Find all customers with a DOB after 1/1/1980. Print the following fields in descending order of **Order Limit**:

**Surname, Order Limit** and **Payment Type**

4   Create a one-to-many relationship between the **Customer ID** field of the **Contact details** table and the **Customer** field of the **Orders** table.

5   Create the following query using the tables **Contact details** and **Orders**:

Find the details of all furniture (F) Item type orders with a price over £10. Print the following fields in ascending order of **Surname**:

**Surname, Initials, Item Description, Price**

6   Delete the query **Pay**.

7   Close the file.

## Exercise 17

*Skills* ◯ Delete relationships between tables

Files required: **artists**

**1** Open the database **artists**.

**2** Delete the relationship between the **Artist ID** on the **Details2** table and the **Artist ID** on the **Works available** table.

**3** Create a one-to-many relationship between the **Artist ID** on the **Artist details** table and the **Artist ID** on the **Works available** table.

**4** Create a query using the tables **Artist details** and **Works available** as follows:

Find all works available by **George Walliams**. Print the following fields in ascending **Price** order:

**Artist-Surname**, **Painting Name** and **Price**.

**5** Close the file.

5

# Section 7 *Consolidation*

## Exercise 18

1 Set up the following database and save as **tours**. Save the table as **outings**. Set the **Code** field as the primary key and index with no duplicates.

| Field Name | Data Type | Field Size or Format |
|---|---|---|
| Code | AutoNumber | |
| Tour | Text | 40 |
| Day | Text | 3 |
| Price (Euros) | Currency | Euro |
| Duration (Hrs) | Number | Long Integer |
| Mode of transport | Text | 20 |

| Code | Tour | Day | Price (Euros) | Duration (Hrs) |
|---|---|---|---|---|
| AutoNumber | Illuminations | Fri | 45 | 2 |
| | Seine Cruise | Tue | 40 | 3 |
| | Marais | Mon | 15 | 2 |

2 Change the width of columns to ensure all data is displayed in full.

3 Sort the data into ascending order of **Price**.

4 In the **Duration** field, set a validation rule to **<4** and validation text **All trips must be less than four hours unless special circumstances.**

5 Print all fields in landscape orientation, setting paper size to *Letter*.

6 Amend the records as follows:

   **Seine Cruise** should be **Wed** and **39 Euros**

7 Add the field **Mode of transport** (Format: Text, field size: 40) and the data as shown.

| Tour | Mode of Transport |
|---|---|
| Illuminations | Open-top bus |
| Seine Cruise | Boat |
| Marais | Foot |

8 Print the **Seine Cruise** record only.

9 Close the file.

## Exercise 19

Files required: **students3**

1   Open the database **students3**.

2   Delete the **Students Accounting** table.

3   Edit the query **Term1** as follows:
    • delete the **Course** field
    • select only courses with a fee of £60 or more
    • hide the fields **DOB** and **Fees**
    • sort in ascending order of **Last name**.

4   Save and print the amended query above.

5   Using the **STUDENTS** table, produce a report as follows:

    • display all the fields except **Student No** and **DOB** and all the records
    • group by **Course**
    • sort in alphabetical order of **Last name**
    • title the report **Autumn Enrolment**
    • add the summary value Average for the **Fees** field
    • add a footer with your name and current time of day in Arial Black, 12 pt.

6   Preview and amend the report as necessary to display all the data.

7   Print the report.

8   Close the file.

## Exercise 20

Files required: **sold**

1   Open the database **sold**.

2   Amend the table **Properties for sale** as follows:
    • delete the field **Viewings**
    • set the **Date Registered** field to **Long Date** format
    • set the **Property Ref** field as the primary key with no duplicates
    • change the field size of **Property Ref** to 4.

3   Amend the record Property Ref. **N654** to have a new price of **£189,000**.

**4** Create the following table and save as **Buyers**. Set the **Property Ref** as the primary key and index with no duplicates.

| Field Name | Data Type | Field Size or Format |
|---|---|---|
| Property Ref | Text | 5 |
| Buyer Surname | Text | 20 |
| Mortgage Required | Yes/No | |

**5** Key in the following data:

| Property Ref | Buyer Surname | Mortgage Required |
|---|---|---|
| N654 | Mr C Dalley | No |
| Y88 | Ms A Heston | Yes |
| W821 | Dr Hartley | Yes |

**6** Using the **Property Ref** fields from the **Buyers** and **Properties for sale** tables, create a one-to-one relationship between the tables.

**7** Apply referential integrity to the relationship.

**8** Using both tables, create the following query with the name **Mortgage**:

Find all properties with **Mortgage Required**. Print the following fields in ascending order of **Date Registered**:

**Location, Price, Date Registered, Buyer Surname**

**9** Close the file.

## Exercise 21

Files required: **hols**

(*Note:* This file has many more records than you will be expected to handle for the ECDL test but it will provide useful practice.)

**1** Open the database **hols**.

**2** Delete the **props old** table.

**3** Working with the **Properties** table:
- delete the **BOOKED(A)**, **BOOKED(B)**, **PRICE CODE**, **CHANGE DAY** and **AGENT** fields
- move the **LOCATION** field so that it comes before the **PROPERTY NAME** field
- use **Find** to locate the property **CODE R567** and delete this record.

**4** Create a simple form using all the fields in the **Props2** table. Save the form as **Sea**.

**5**  Apply a filter to find all properties with TV and note down the names of the properties found. Remove the filter.

**6**  Working with the form:

Find and amend the record for **Property Name NIMBUS** to **Code S777**. Add a new record as follows:

| Property Name | Code | Occupants | Bedrooms | Pets | TV | Price Code |
|---|---|---|---|---|---|---|
| Mayflies | S990 | 2 | 1 | No | No | B |

**7**  Print only the new record in Form format.

**8**  Close the form.

**9**  Open the table **Props2,** sort into alphabetical order of **Property Name** and print all records and fields.

**10**  Delete the form **Props 2004.**

**11**  Close the file.

**5**

## Exercise 22

**1**  Explain how you do the following:
- look for information using Access Help
- modify the Access toolbar
- use **Undo/Redo**.

**2**  Explain what is meant by relational databases. Why is it useful to be able to relate tables in a database? What sort of rules need to be set and why?

**3**  What is a primary key?

**4**  When would you use indexing?

**5**  You have just changed the size of a field in an existing database table. What might the consequences be?

# Presentation

**Module 6**

## Section

Please note that many skills are expanded upon and duplicated throughout the exercises.

6

# Section 1  *Getting started*

## Exercise 1

| Skills | |
|---|---|
| ○ | Open/close application |
| ○ | Create a new presentation |
| ○ | Apply automatic slide layout |
| ○ | Add text |
| ○ | Apply text formatting: bold, italic, underline |
| ○ | Apply case changes to text |
| ○ | Change text appearance: font sizes, font type |
| ○ | Apply colour to text |
| ○ | Save a presentation |
| ○ | Print slides in various views |

**1**  Start the presentation application and create the following three-slide presentation:

*Slide 1* (use **Title Only** AutoLayout)

**British Television**

*Slide 2* (use **Title and Text** AutoLayout)

1960s

- Sunday Palladium
- Take Your Pick
- Emergency Ward Ten

*Slide 3* (use **Title and Text** AutoLayout)

1970s

- This is Your Life
- Sale of the Century
- Morecambe and Wise

**2**  Save the presentation as **TV.ppt**.

**3**  On slide 1, automatically change the text to upper case. Increase the font size by 2 pt and change the font type to **Century Gothic**.

**4**  On slide 2, embolden the text **Take Your Pick**. Underline the text **Sunday Palladium**.

**5**  On slide 3, colour the text **Sale of the Century** in green. Italicise the text **This is Your Life**.

**6**  Save the presentation as **TV2.ppt** and print as slides.

**7**  Close the presentation.

**8**  Close the application.

## Exercise 2

| | |
|---|---|
| *Skills* | ○ Add an image: resize and move |
| | ○ Apply shadow to text |
| | ○ Adjust line spacing |
| | ○ Change type of bullets |
| | ○ Select appropriate output |

**1**  Create the following four-slide presentation. Format it to good effect using the layout below to guide you.

*Slide 1*

Use **Title Only** AutoLayout.

> **Special Branch Gardens**

*Slide 2*

Use **Title Slide** AutoLayout. Apply shadow to the **Garden Design and Construction** text.

> **Special Branch Gardens**
>
> Garden Design and Construction
>
> Tel: 0117 710710
>
> *E-mail: sbl@example.com*

*Slide 3*

Use **Title and Text** AutoLayout. Format the bullets as hollow circles. Insert a suitable piece of clip art in the bottom left corner and resize so that it is 3.25 cm high and 4.25 cm wide.

> **We Provide:**
> ○ Professionally drawn plans
> ○ Free itemised quotations
> ○ Portfolio of previous work and client references

*Slide 4*

Use **Title and Text over Content** AutoLayout. Adjust the line spacing in the text to 1.50 lines. *Note*: Delete the bullets by selecting them and pressing **Delete**.

---

**Taking Bookings for Spring**

We can transform your garden from an untidy yard or rambling wilderness to an enchanting place to relax and unwind. Our enthusiasm knows no bounds!

Insert suitable clip art here

---

**2**  Automatically change the title text on slide 2 to upper case.

**3**  Apply shadow to the text on slide 1.

**4**  Proofread and use the spellcheck to ensure accuracy.

**5**  Save the presentation as **landscapes.ppt** and print as handouts with 4 slides per page.

## Exercise 3

*Skills*
- ◯ Change **View** modes
- ◯ Resize and move text within a slide
- ◯ Apply design template

**1**  Create a three-slide presentation with the following attributes:

*Slide 1* (use **Title Slide** AutoLayout)

**PowerPoint Info**

**(Your name)**

*Slide 2* (use **Title and Text** AutoLayout)

**Slide Views**
- Normal
- Slide Sorter
- Slide Show

*Slide 3* (use **Title and Text** AutoLayout)
Getting Help Help menu
- Search for
- Table of Contents
- Office Online

**2**  Save the presentation as **power talk.ppt**.

**3**  Print as handouts with 3 slides per page.

**4**  Apply the **Eclipse** design template to all slides. Switch to **Slide Show** view and view the presentation.

**5**  Change to the **Crayons** design template and apply to all slides. Switch to **Slide Show** view and view the presentation.

**6**  On slide 3, move the text box **Getting Help Help menu** so that it appears at the bottom of the list. Change the font size of the moved text so it is smaller than that in the list above it.

**7**  Adjust the line spacing of the bulleted list to 1.3 lines.

**8**  Change the layout of slide 1 to **Title Only**.

**9**  Save the file as **talk2.ppt** and print slide 1 and slide 3 only as handouts, 3 per page.

**10**  Close the file.

6

## Exercise 4

*Skills*  ◯ Align text: centre, left, right, top, bottom
◯ Modify slide layout

**1**  Create the following presentation. Format it to good effect.

*Slide 1* (use **Title Slide** AutoLayout)
**Keynes Veterinary Clinic**
**Choosing a Healthy Kitten**

*Slide 2* (use **Title Slide** AutoLayout)
**Never give as a present**
**A cat is for life**

*Slide 3* (use **Title and Text** AutoLayout)

Types:

- Longhair
- Shorthair

*Slide 4* (use **Title and Text** AutoLayout)

Look for:

- Bright, clear eyes
- Dry, clean tail
- Clean ears

2  Apply a light green background to all slides.

3  Set all title text to dark blue.

4  Right-align the subtitle text on slide 2.

5  Left-align the title text on slide 1.

6  Insert a text box to slide 1 with the text **animal welfare 2007**, formatted as Times New Roman, 16 pt, Bold and align it at the bottom centre of the slide.

7  Centre the listed text on slide 4.

8  Insert the text **Healthy coat** on slide 4 between **Dry, clean tail** and **Clean ears**.

9  Save the presentation as **cat.ppt.**

10  Print as handouts, 2 per page and close.

# Section 2 *Editing and refining*

## Exercise 5

| Skills | Open an existing presentation<br>Save an existing presentation |
| --- | --- |

Files required: **cat.ppt** (saved in Exercise 4)

1  Open the file **cat.ppt** saved in Exercise 4.

2  Change the background to light blue on all slides.

3  Resave with the same filename **cat.ppt**.

4  On slide 2, add the text **surprise** so the sentence reads **Never give as a surprise present**.

5  Insert a suitable piece of clip art to slide 2.

6  Save as **cat2**, print slide 2 only and close.

## Exercise 6

| Skills | Add lines, move lines, change line colour and width<br>Add shapes and free-drawn lines<br>Rotate or flip an object<br>Change attributes: colour, line type, apply shadow |
| --- | --- |

Files required: **shapes.ppt**

1  Open the file **shapes.ppt**.

2  On slide 1, insert your name where shown then underline and right-align this text.

**6**

**3** On slide 2:

- change the colour of the arrow to green and enlarge it so that it is approximately twice as big
- flip the clip art vertically so it is the correct way up
- rotate the triangle left 90 degrees, change its line type to 2 pt, apply shadow Style 10
- move the face so that it is sitting on the line below it
- copy the face, place the copy next to the original and colour it purple.

**4** On slide 3:

- change the length of the top line so that it is the same length as the others
- change the dotted line to Dash Dot, and its colour to blue
- delete the red line
- insert a new line with a width of 10 cm, coloured green, 4 pt, Arrow Style 9, to become the top line
- insert a new line to become the bottom line with a width of 5 cm, coloured red, 6 pt, set the arrow Begin style to Oval arrow and the arrow End style to Stealth arrow.

**5** On slide 4, insert the following diagram:

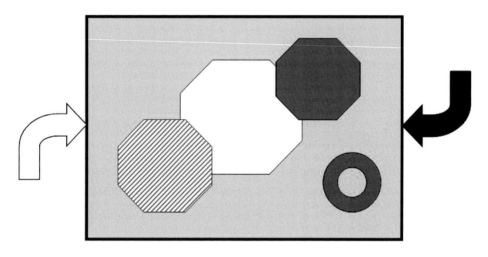

**6** On slide 5:

- resize the grouped shapes to 8.74 cm wide by 10.5 cm high and centre on the slide
- ungroup the shapes and delete one of the tall trees
- colour all the pots black
- add a Freeform wavy line under the pots.

**7** Save the file as **shapesfun.ppt** and print as handouts, 6 per page.

**8** Close the file.

## Exercise 7

*Skills*      Add notes to slides

Files required: **images.ppt**

**1** Open the file **images.ppt**.

**2** Add the following notes to slides:

*Slide 10* **Use this image if approval is given at the Friday meeting**
*Slide 4* **This is the second preference image**

**3** Save the file as **images checked.ppt**.

**4** Print slides 4 and 10 together with the notes.

**5** Close the file.

## Exercise 8

*Skills*      Set line weights, style, colours in a textbox

Files required: **fashion.ppt**

**1** Open the file **fashion.ppt**.

**2** On slide 3:
- change the width of the textbox containing the bulleted list so that it takes up only half of the slide
- insert the image **model1.gif** and place it on the right of the slide. Resize it so that it is the same height as the textbox to its left. Ensure that you maintain the aspect ratio (proportions).

**3** On slide 1:
- change the title textbox colour to blue
- change the line colour of this textbox to red and 6 pt.

**4** Save the file as **fash2**.

**5** Print as handouts, 4 per page.

**6** Close the file.

## Exercise 9

*Skills*  ◯ **Create and use a master slide**
◯ **Delete an image/selected text**
◯ **Use Zoom**

Files required: **induction.ppt**

**1** Open the file **induction.ppt**.

**2** Zoom the presentation in **Normal** view to 81%.

**3** Create a master slide for the presentation as follows:
- delete the picture
- add the image **deer.jpg** so that it appears at the bottom left of every slide
- resize the image to 4 cm high and 5.3 cm wide
- add a footer with the date (that updates automatically) and the text **Amended by (yr name)**. Do not display the footer on the Title slide
- apply automatic slide numbering.

**4** On slide 1, enter the current year after the word **Autumn**.

**5** On slide 2, delete the word **permanent**.

**6** Save the file as **training.ppt**.

**7** Print as handouts, 4 per page, and close.

## Exercise 10

*Skills*   ◯ Delete slides
◯ Number slides
◯ Reorder slides

Files required: **hotel.ppt**

1 Open the file **hotel.ppt**.

2 Move slide 3 so that it becomes the fifth slide of the presentation.

3 Insert slide numbers on all slides.

4 Delete slide 2.

5 Save as **hotel1** and print slides as handouts, 6 per page.

6 Close the file.

## Exercise 11

*Skills*   ◯ Use **Copy/Cut and Paste** to duplicate slides/text/
images within a presentation
◯ Work in Outline View

Files required: **sleep.ppt**

1 Open the file **sleep.ppt**.

2 Spellcheck and save as **sleep2.ppt**.

3 Edit the notes for slide 2 to read 12 minutes and not 20.

4 Copy slide 1 so that it also appears as the final slide.

5 Work in Outline View and make the following amendments:
  • on slide 3, cut the text **Expend fewer calories** and paste it on slide 4
    after **Slows down**
  • on slide 2, add the text **most effective** in the sentence after the word
    **their** and before the word **at**
  • on slide 3, add the word **fall** after **Adrenaline levels.**

**6**    Copy the picture on slide 1 so that it appears on slide 2 at the bottom left.

**7**    Save the file as **sleep3.ppt**.

**8**    Print in Outline View.

**9**    Print slide 2 only as a Notes page.

**10**    Change to portrait display and print slide 3 only in slide view.

**11**    Save the file.

## Exercise 12

> *Skills*
> - Open several presentations
> - Use **Copy/Cut and Paste** to duplicate slides/text/images between open presentations
> - Save under a different file format or version number

Files required: **learn pp.ppt**
                    **venues.ppt**

**1**    Open the file **learn pp.ppt** and change the design template to **Echo**.

**2**    Open the file **venues.ppt** and insert the current year on slide 1.

**3**    Switch to the **learn pp** presentation and copy the computer picture from slide 1 to slide 1 of the **venues** presentation.

**4**    Copy slide 1 of the **venues** presentation to become slide 1 of a new file.

**5**    Save the new presentation in RTF (Rich Text Format) as **venues1.rtf** to a floppy disk.

**6**    Switch to the **learn pp** presentation and copy the text on slide 2 to slide 3 of the **venues** presentation.

**7**    In the **venues** presentation, create a footer **Learning venues** and display it on all slides except the **Title** slide.

**8**    Save the venues file as **venues2.ppt**. Save the new file as **new training.ppt**.

**9**    Quick save all other files.

**10**    Print all the files as handouts, 6 per page.

**11**    Close all files.

# Section 3 *Working with charts*

## Exercise 13

**1** Open a new file and select the **Title and Diagram or Organization Chart** AutoLayout.

**2** Key in the title **Current Staff** in the Title placeholder.

**3** Enter the organisational chart details as below:

**4** Save the presentation as **org chart** and print the slide.

**5** Close the presentation.

6

## Exercise 14

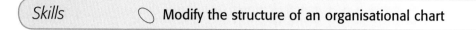

*Skills*          Modify the structure of an organisational chart

Files required: **org chart.ppt** (saved in Exercise 13)

**1**   Open the file **org chart.ppt** saved in Exercise 13.

**2**   Copy the chart to a new slide 2. Change the title of slide 2 to **Old Staff Structure**.

**3**   On slide 1, make amendments to the organisational chart as follows:
- **Dr Ron Jones** replaces **Prof Oliver Malinski** as Head of Fine Art
- delete **Dr Ron Jones, Senior Lecturer** box
- insert **Ms April Smythe, Senior Lecturer**, a new co-worker of Mr David Blair
- remove **Dr Thusitha Uhiari, Head of Photography** box.

**4**   Save the file as **amended org.ppt**.

**5**   Print slide 1 and close.

## Exercise 15

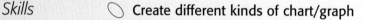

*Skills*          Create different kinds of chart/graph

**1**   Open a new presentation and use **Title and Chart** AutoLayout.

**2**   Add the title **Student Numbers**.

**3**   Use the following information to produce a 3-D column chart.

|        | Art | Text | Graphics |
|--------|-----|------|----------|
| Unit 1 | 20  | 25   | 21       |
| Unit 2 | 24  | 19   | 18       |
| Unit 3 | 10  | 12   | 16       |

**4**   Save as **chart.ppt** and print slide 1.

**5**   Copy the chart to a new blank slide 2 in the presentation.

**6**   Insert a new blank slide 3.

**7**   Insert a textbox at the top of slide 3 with the text **Department Numbers**.

**8** Change the chart on slide 1 to a Clustered Bar type.

**9** Amend the figures for **Art** as follows: **Unit 1: 25, Unit 2: 20, Unit 3: 20**.

**10** Change the background colour of the chart to yellow.

**11** Change the colour of the bars for **Unit 1** to red.

**12** Move the chart on slide 2 to slide 3.

**13** Delete slide 2.

**14** Save as **chart3**, print as handouts, 2 per page and close.

## Exercise 16

**1** Open a new presentation and use **Title and Chart** AutoLayout.

**2** Add the title **Art Courses – Average Grades**.

**3** Use the following information to produce a line graph of the average assignment grades for the three units for Art courses:

| Unit 1 | Unit 2 | Unit 3 |
|--------|--------|--------|
| 64     | 53     | 68     |

**4** Delete the legend.

**5** Change the background colour of the graph to green.

**6** Save the presentation as **art average.ppt** and print slide 1.

**7** Change the chart to an exploded pie with 3-D visual effect.

**8** Change the colour of the pie slice for Unit 3 to red.

**9** Display data labels with category name and value next to the slices.

**10** Save as **art pie.ppt** and print slide 1.

**11** Close the file.

6

# Section 4 *Automating a presentation*

### Exercise 17

| Skills | ○ Add slide transitions, timings and effects |
|---|---|
| | ○ Start a slide show |
| | ○ Unhide slide |

Files required: **show.ppt**

1 Open the file **show.ppt**.

2 Change the lists on slides 2 and 3 to numbered.

3 Add a piece of clip art (fruit or vegetable) to slide 4.

4 Delete the picture on slide 2.

5 Add slide numbers to all slides.

6 Unhide slide 2 and view the slides in Slide Show view.

7 Move slide 4 so that it is the last slide in the presentation.

8 Apply a transition timing and effect (apply the effect to all slides – you can select an effect or accept the default) between all the slides in the presentation as follows:

| Slide number | Slide duration |
|---|---|
| Slide 1 | 3 sec |
| Slide 2 | 5 sec |
| Slide 3 | 6 sec |
| Slide 4 | 6 sec |
| Slide 5 | 10 sec |

9 View the slide show from slide 3.

10 Now view the slide show from slide 1.

11 Save the presentation as **show1.ppt**.

12 Print as handouts, 6 per page.

13 Close the file.

## Exercise 18

*Skills*
- Add preset animation effects
- Change preset animation effects
- Hide slide

Files required: **show1.ppt** (saved in Exercise 17)

1 Open the file **show1.ppt** (saved in Exercise 17).

2 Change the transitional timing of slide 2 to 6 sec.

3 Change the transitional effect on slide 4 to a different effect.

4 Add preset animation effects to all slides except slide 3.

5 View the slide show.

6 Now hide slide 2 and add an animation effect to slide 3.

7 View the show.

8 Save the file as **showdone.ppt**.

9 Close the file.

**6**

# Section 5 *Consolidation*

## Exercise 19

Create the following three-page presentation.

1　For the first slide, use **Title Slide** AutoLayout. Key in the text **Autocentre Aces** as the title and **Open Every Day** as the subtitle.

2　On the master slide, create a footer with your name and date, set at **14 October 2006**. Apply to all slides.

3　Insert a suitable piece of clip art on the master slide. Resize and position it at the bottom right so that it looks effective.

4　On slide 2, key in the text **Servicing**.

5　Underneath, key in the following bulleted list:

- Up to 1300cc ONLY £69.95
- Up to 1600cc ONLY £79.95
- Up to 2000cc ONLY 89.95
- Up to 2500cc ONLY 99.95

6　Format the bullets as squares.

7　Insert a Long Dash line, 2¼ pt coloured red across the slide below the list.

8　Below the line, create a textbox and add the text **50% off MOT test when booked with any service**.

9　On slide 3, create an organisational chart entitled **Meet the Team** as follows:

Brian Harris – Managing Director, Jay Quinn and Kiki Green are Managers immediately subordinate to Brian Harris. Greg Barton is the Supervisor subordinate to Jay Quinn. Aled Watts and Kay Jones are Mechanics subordinate to Greg Barton.

10　Apply a template design that you think will look appropriate.

11　Save the presentation as **autocentre.ppt** and print slides as handouts, three per page.

## Exercise 20

Files required: **good bad.ppt**

1   Open the file **good bad.ppt**.

2   Spellcheck and save as **good1.ppt**.

3   On the final slide, change the text of the last two sentences to sentence case.

4   Replace the word **capital** with **upper** throughout.

5   On slide 7, embolden the text **What do you think?**

6   Add the following text to the note on slide 3:
    **Demonstration that lower case looks better.**

7   Apply a custom colour scheme to all slides: **Background:** Blue, **Title Text:** Black, **Text and Line:** White.

8   Enter the text **and easier to read** on slide 6 after the word **restful**. Ensure that the text is centred in this placeholder then set its background colour to light green and its font colour to red.

9   On the master slide, change the footer to display an automatic today's date, replace the name in **amended by** with your name. Display the footer on all slides (including the **Title** slide).

10  Delete slide 9.

11  Duplicate slide 1 to the end of the presentation.

12  Resave the presentation.

13  Save another version of the file as **good2** in RTF (Rich Text Format).

14  Print as handouts, 6 per page.

15  Print slide 3 only as a Notes page.

16  Close the presentation.

## Exercise 21

Files required: **art.ppt**

1   Open the presentation **art.ppt**.

2   Format and amend slide 2 as follows:
    • change the background colour to yellow
    • add shadow to the title text and increase its size by 6 pt

6

- change the colour of the squares to blue
- bring the triangle to the front and fill it with a green dot pattern
- enlarge the moon shape so that it is twice as big and rotate it left by 90 degrees.

**3** Create a new slide after slide 1 using the **Title and Chart** AutoLayout.

**4** Insert the title **Genre Preference**. Add a column bar chart using the data below:

|  | Poll 1 | Poll 2 | Poll 3 |
|---|---|---|---|
| Landscape | 5 | 3 | 7 |
| Still Life | 6 | 7 | 5 |
| Portrait | 4 | 5 | 3 |

**5** Colour the bars as follows:

**Landscape: Red, Still Life: Green, Portrait: Yellow**

**6** Add a Box Out transition effect to slide 2 and an automatic timing of 4 sec.

**7** Change the timing of slide 1 to 6 sec.

**8** View the slide show.

**9** Save the file as **art genres.ppt**.

**10** Print as slides, each on its own page.

**11** Close the file.

## Exercise 22

**1** Use your creative skills to create a five-page presentation (save as **mydesign.ppt**) about a place that you know. This could be your home town or a place that you like to visit. Include pictures or images.

**2** Open any other file that you have saved previously and copy a picture or image from your new presentation to the older file.

**3** Open a new file and copy the picture or image to slide 1 of the new file.

**4** Save the files opened at steps 2 and 3 using the names **clip1** and **clip2** where appropriate.

**5** Resave the **mydesign.ppt** file.

**6** Close all files except the one that you have designed.

**7** Show this as a slide show to someone you know so that they can comment on its effectiveness.

**8** Make amendments as appropriate.

**9** Close the file.

## Exercise 23

*Skills*
- ◯ Use application help functions
- ◯ Modify toolbar display
- ◯ Modify basic options/preferences
- ◯ Use **Undo/Redo**

**1** Use your creative skills to create a five-page presentation about PowerPoint.

**2** Save as **me as tutor.ppt**.

**3** Use the **Title Slide** AutoLayout for slide 1. Enter a suitable title and your name.

**4** Use the **Title and Text** AutoLayout for slides 2 to 5.

**5** On slide 2, enter a suitable title and a few brief bullet points about modifying the toolbar display.

**6** On slide 3, enter a suitable title and a few brief bullet points about how to change basic options: user name and default folder for opening/saving presentations.

**7** On slide 4, enter a suitable title and few brief bullet points about using **Undo/Redo**.

**8** On slide 5, enter a few bullet points about how to use PowerPoint Help. Copy and paste a sentence from a Help topic to slide 5.

**9** Apply a design template.

**10** Insert a suitable piece of clip art into slide 1 and resize as appropriate.

**11** Resave the presentation.

**12** View in Slide View.

**13** Print as handouts, 6 per page.

**14** Close the file.

6

# Information and communication

**Module 7**

7

## Section

Please note that many skills are expanded upon and duplicated throughout the exercises.

*Note:* Answers are provided for Exercise 12 only.

# Section 1 *Getting started with the World Wide Web*

### Exercise 1

| Skills | |
|---|---|
| *Skills* | ◯ Open a web-browsing application |
| | ◯ Display a given web page |
| | ◯ Change the web browser home page |
| | ◯ Display a web page in a new window |
| | ◯ Save a web page/picture as a file |
| | ◯ Display/hide images on a web page |
| | ◯ Close the web-browsing application |

**1** Open a web browser.

**2** Check the address of your current home page (its URL is displayed in the address box) and copy this address to a new Word document. Save the Word document as **web stuff**.

**3** Display the home page of the 2012 Olympics:

www.london2012.org

**4** Display the ITN home page in a new window:

www.itn.co.uk

**5** Examine the home pages above and decide what you like/do not like about them. Switch to the **web stuff** Word document and make a note of your opinion of their main good points and their main bad points.

**6** Set one of the site's (2012 Olympics or ITN) home pages as your web browser home page.

**7** Save the 2012 Olympics web page as a file in TXT format.

**8** Save the ITN web page as a file in HTML format.

**9** Save one of the images only from the web pages.

**10** Paste the saved image into the Word document.

**11** Change the browser's settings so that images are not loaded.

**12** Display the following website home page:

www.allmusic.com

**13**  Change the browser's settings so that images are displayed.

**14**  Copy the **All Music Guide** web address to the Word document created at step 2 and save.

**15**  Exit Word.

**16**  Exit the browser.

7

# Section 2 *Browsing and Favorites*

## Exercise 2

> *Skills*
> ○ Navigate using hyperlinks
> ○ Stop a web page from downloading
> ○ Work with Favorites
> ○ Display previously visited pages
> ○ Delete browser history

**1** Open a web browser.

**2** Stop your home page from downloading.

**3** Access a few of the sites listed below (depending on your interests):

| | |
|---|---|
| London Visitor Information | www.visitlondon.com |
| Radio 1 | www.bbc.co.uk/radio1 |
| Radio 4 | www.bbc.co.uk/radio4 |
| UK Comedy Guide | www.chortle.co.uk |
| Wales Tourist Board | www.visitwales.com |
| Football365 | www.football365.com |
| Tate Liverpool | www.tate.org.uk/liverpool |
| The Foody Recipes | www.thefoody.com |
| How Stuff Works | www.howstuffworks.com |
| Children's BBC | www.bbc.co.uk/cbbc |
| British Space Centre | www.bnsc.gov.uk |
| The Mirror | www.mirror.co.uk |
| The Times | www.the-times.co.uk |

**4** Using hyperlinks, find out some information that is not available on their home pages.

**5** Practise navigating backwards and forwards between pages, noticing how the URL in the address box changes.

**6** Click on the drop-down menu of the browser address bar to display previously visited URLs.

**7** Add the home page of a few of the websites above, that you find interesting, to your **Favorites** in a folder with the name **ECDL prac**.

**8** Return to your home page.

**9** Delete one of your **Favorites**.

**10** Display one of your **Favorites**.

**11** Delete the browser history.

# Section 3 *Searching*

## Exercise 3

> *Skills*
> ◌ Use search engines
> ◌ Print a web page

1 Using a search engine or search directory, find answers to the questions below and:
  - record how many hits you have for each search
  - practise refining the searches to have fewer hits and more relevant information
  - try changing search engines and directories to determine which give the best results.

  a What is on BBC Radio 4 at 8 pm this evening?
  b How old were these artists when they died: John Constable, Mark Rothko, Salvador Dali?
  c Who invented the crossword and when?
  d What is the population of the Isle of Man?
  e What is the wingspan of an eagle owl?
  f Find a photo of an eagle owl, save it to your own work area and print it.
  g What time do flights depart from London (Luton) airport tomorrow morning (leaving at approximately 10 am) destination Nice? How much would a return fare be if returning after three nights in Nice?
  h What is the current most popular choice of first name for girls/boys?
  i What is the address of Leicester City Football Club?
  j Who won the Wimbledon Singles Tennis championship in 1988 (Ladies' and Men's)?
  k When were the following musicians born: Mozart, John Lennon, Vivaldi?
  l What is the current Bank of England interest rate?

2 Print out the results of your searches, detailing the information requested and using **Preview** before printing. Choose output carefully to include only the information requested. Select from: entire web page, specific page(s), specific frame and selected text.

3 Practise changing page margins, orientation, paper size and number of pages for printing.

## Exercise 4

*Skills*  ◯ **Completing a web-based form**

Web-based forms can usually be found on sites that have something to sell. For example, you can fill out a form to arrange for a brochure to be sent to your address, check the availability of accommodation, arrange flights or register to order groceries online.

**NB:** This is a practice task only. You do not need to proceed after completing the first page of the form. DO NOT ENTER ANY CREDIT CARD DETAILS.

Access a few different websites using a search to find suitable ones and practise completing web-based forms.

7

# Section 4 *Getting started with e-mail*

### Exercise 5

| *Skills* | |
|---|---|
| | ○ Open an e-mail application |
| | ○ Create a new message |
| | ○ Use a spellchecking tool |
| | ○ Send a message with low/high priority |
| | ○ Copy/blind copy a message to another address |
| | ○ Receive messages |
| | ○ Close an e-mail application |

**1**   Open an e-mail application.

**2**   Prepare the following message to send to someone you know, copy (use Cc) to someone else and blind copy (Bcc) to a third person.

**3**   Give the message the subject **Badminton**.

**4**   Ensure that you check spelling before sending and send with the priority set to high.

Hello (recipient's name)

Badminton Club will not be meeting at lunchtime today due to exams taking place in the Sports Hall. However, I have been informed that the hall is free this evening. Are you able to meet up then?

Regards

(Your name)

# Section 5 *Organising messages*

## Exercise 6

*Skills*
- Open a mail message
- Attach a file to a message
- Delete text in a message
- Delete a file attachment from a message
- Open and save a document
- Use reply to sender/reply to all
- Reply with/without original message insertion
- Forward a message
- Use **Cut/Copy** and **Paste/Delete**
- Create a new mail folder
- Delete a message
- Sort messages by name, subject, date, etc.
- Move messages to a new mail folder
- Flag a message in a mail folder
- Search for a message
- Mark a message as unread

**7**

Files required: **poetry.doc**

1 Preview and print a received message.

2 Select a section of text from a received message and print two copies of the selection.

3 Reply to any message you have received, with original message insertion (use **Reply to Sender/Reply to All** as appropriate).

4 Reply to any message you have received, deleting original message insertion (use **Reply to Sender/Reply to All** as appropriate).

5 Access any received message and forward it to someone.

6 Access another received message and mark it as unread.

7 Copy one sentence from a received message to a new e-mail message.

8 Set the subject of the new message to **Poetry**.

9 Attach the Word file **Poetry**.

**10** For practice purposes, delete the attachment and then re-attach it.

**11** Send the message to someone and a copy to someone else.

**12** Save any received e-mail to a folder named **Prac (yr name)**.

**13** Save a received attachment to your own work area.

**14** Look for all messages from a particular person using **Find**, **Message**.

**15** Sort your e-mails into Subject order.

**16** Delete an old message that you don't want to keep.

**17** Restore the message above from the **Deleted items** folder.

**18** Empty the **Deleted items** folder.

**19** Delete one sentence from an old message.

**20** Flag one of your messages.

# Section 6 *The Address Book*

## Exercise 7

*Skills*
- Add a mail address to an address list
- Delete a mail address from an address list
- Create a new address list/distribution list
- Send a message using a distribution list

**1**  Add the following address to the **Address Book**:

Jake Wilde
j.p.k.wilde@example.com

**2**  Delete one of the names in your **Address Book**.

**3**  Set up a new group called **Ice Hockey**. Include the following in the group:

Jake Wilde and two other contacts in your address book

**4**  Send a message to the **Ice Hockey** mailing list with the title **Friendly** as follows:

Date for your diary
Mid-winter friendly
The date has now been fixed for the first Saturday in December.
After match social is 'Curry at The Bear's Arms'.
Your name

**5**  Delete **Jake Wilde** from the **Ice Hockey** list.

**6**  Close the e-mail application.

7

# Section 7 *Consolidation*

For Exercises 8 and 9 you will be working on a fictitious scenario.

## Exercise 8

Your company is planning to offer a day trip to an amusement park as first prize in a competition and you need to find out information and costings. The two venues currently being considered are Alton Towers, UK, and Disneyland – Paris, France.

1   Open a web browser.

2   Delete the **History** from the browser.

3   Search the Internet to find the sites for **Alton Towers** and **Disneyland – Paris**.

4   Add both sites to your Favorites.

5   Find out the prices for a one-day pass for an adult and for a child at each venue. Make a note of these prices.

6   Open your e-mail application and prepare a message with the title **Prizes** to your manager, and Cc it to another colleague:

   **Manager's name**
   **Here are the web addresses of the amusement parks:**
   **(Paste the addresses here** (copied from the browser **Address** bar))
   **Costs for one-day passes:**
   **Alton Towers: Adult: (insert price); Child: (insert price)**
   **Disneyland – Paris: Adult: (insert price); Child: (insert price)**
   **Your name**

7   Spellcheck and send the e-mail.

8   Access the **Alton Towers** site again, using **Favorites**.

9   Find a map of directions if travelling by road.

10   Save the map to your own work area and print it.

11   Look for a photo of one of the main attractions at Alton Towers.

12   Open a Word document and save as **Amusements**.

13   Paste the picture located in step 10 into the Word document, resizing as necessary.

**14** Access the **Disneyland – Paris** site again. Copy a few lines of text from this site to your **Amusements** document that would be useful if travelling there by train.

**15** Resave and close the **Amusements** file.

**16** To help with decision making, it would be useful to know the currency conversion rates (UK £ against the euro). Search for this information and make a note of today's rate.

## Exercise 9

Files required: **Amusements.doc** (saved in Exercise 8)

**1** Open your e-mail application and prepare the following e-mail with the subject **First prize**:

Hello Drew

As you know, we are hoping to offer a trip as first prize in the competition. In order for you to make a start on the promotional material, you may find the information in the attached file useful.

Best wishes
(Your name)

**2** Attach the file **Amusements.doc** (saved in Exercise 8).

**3** Send the e-mail to your colleague with priority set to low.

**4** Close your e-mail application.

7

# Section 8 *Knowledge test – WWW*

## Exercise 10

1   Explain what a web browser is and why you would use it?

2   What do the initials http stand for?

3   Explain what is meant by a browser's cache.

4   Give an example of a (real or made up) commercial web address and explain how each part is derived.

5   What is another name for a web address?

6   Explain what a hyperlink is.

7   What do the initials FTP stand for?

8   Explain how you would download a file from a web page to your hard disk?

9   What is encryption and when is it used?

10   'Home page' can have two different meanings. Explain.

11   Explain the differences between the Internet and the World Wide Web (WWW).

12   When completing a web-based form, which symbol is used to denote mandatory entries?

13   Why might passwords be used when accessing the Internet?

14   Explain why a cookie might save you time and effort.

15   Which options might you deselect to load a web page more quickly?

16   When using the **Help** menu, what options do you have for finding help topics?

17   Explain how a search engine would help you find information on the web.

18   When undertaking a search, what is a key word?

**19** Why should you be careful when downloading files from the Internet?

**20** Why would you subscribe to an ISP? What do the initials ISP stand for?

**21** Why do organisations and individuals install firewall software?

**22** What precautions should you take before purchasing from a website?

**23** Explain the function of digital certificates in relation to Internet fraud.

**24** Name two commonly used web browsers.

**25** Explain the purpose of the **Refresh** button?

**26** What do the initials URL stand for and why are some longer than others?

**27** What pointer symbol is used to denote that you have placed it over a hyperlink?

**28** Explain the function of **Favorites (Bookmarks)**.

**29** How would you change the look of a web page to suit your needs (colours, fonts etc.) and remove the toolbar?

7

# Section 9 *Knowledge test – e-mail*

## Exercise 11

**1**   What does using capital letters in e-mail denote?

**2**   What is meant by netiquette?

**3**   What is spam?

**4**   What can you do reduce to reduce the risk of receiving a virus via e-mail?

**5**   In e-mail, how would you automatically update an **Address Book** from incoming mail?

**6**   How do you display/hide built-in toolbars?

**7**   What advantage might there be in reading and writing e-mails offline?

**8**   Explain the makeup of the following e-mail address:

p.nut@example.com

**9**   Explain some steps you can take to manage your e-mail.

**10**   How do you access **Help** when using your e-mail application?

**11**   How do you customise the **Inbox** headings, e.g. **Sender**, **Subject**, **Date received**?

# Section 10 *Crossword*

## Exercise 12

## Across

1. Junk mail (4)
2. Used to display a web page quickly (5)
4. Mark as __ to make your message look as if it still hasn't been read (6)
8. If there was a finishing school for web users, they would teach this subject (10)
10. Name of popular search directory (5)
12. First page of a website (4)
13. Location for storing messages on arrival (5)
14. Symbol associated with hyperlink (4)
18. Name of organisation in web address (6)
21. Sites found that contain your key words (4)
22. Location for storing messages before sending them (6)
24. A popular search engine (6)
25. Press this button to update (7)
26. State of being connected to Internet (6)
27. (A cloth-like item) reminds you that an e-mail needs attention (4)
28. Type of website having .ac in its URL (8)

## Down

1. A way of viewing the whole page (9)
3. High-speed way to jump between web pages (9)
5. The default symbol for this is a paperclip (10)
6. Type of word used by a search engine (3)
7. Button for moving ahead (7)
9. You keep returning to these sites [U.S.] (9)
11. Surfers and spiders spend time on it (3)
15. How you move around a website (8)
16. Post via the Internet (5)
17. The P in FTP (8)
19. Websites can put these on your computer to save your previous settings (7)
20. A virus has difficulty climbing over them (9)
23. Computers can work when disconnected like this, but not railway trains (7)

# Using IT

## Section

**1** General questions

**2** Multiple-choice questions

**3** Crossword

*Note:* Answers to the Multiple-choice questions and Crossword sections can be found on the CD-ROM.

E

# Section 1 *General questions*

## Exercise 1

**1**  Many organisations have a standard design for their documents (e.g. layout, font type/size and logo). Explain the advantages of this approach.

**2**  Why is it important to regularly update a computer virus checker?

**3**  In the commonly used 'family' method of storing backup files, which male represents the current version?

**4**  Describe some advantages to be gained from deleting obsolete files.

**5**  Why is it preferable to use codes for data entry?

**6**  What type of file has the extension .exe?

**7**  Give an example of how the **Copy**, **Cut** and **Paste** functions might be used.

**8**  Name an internationally recognised computer qualification.

**9**  List the three offences specified in the Computer Misuse Act (1990).

**10**  Describe the data security issues related to the disposal of obsolete or faulty computers.

## Exercise 2

**1**  When information is linked between applications it may lose its original format. What name covers the range of functions available for recovery?

**2**  Where in Windows would you look for the power management options?

**3**  What are the advantages of using the **Search** and **Replace** functions over manual methods?

**4**  Describe copyright issues that relate to downloading material from the Internet.

**5**  What type of chart would best illustrate trends in data?

**6**  What is a graphical user interface (GUI)? Describe some of the advantages of this software design approach.

**7**  List the three main components of a desktop computer system.

**8** What is the most common unit of storage for a modern hard disk: megabyte, gigabyte or terabyte?

**9** Compared with an older film camera, what advantages and disadvantages might a digital version have?

**10** Which are the most appropriate applications software packages to use for the following tasks?

   **a** Editing images.

   **b** Calculating expenditure.

   **c** Producing a brochure.

   **d** Producing a letter.

   **e** Filing customer details.

   **f** Searching for information on the Internet.

## Exercise 3

**1** How could you participate in e-commerce and what might be the advantages and disadvantages of electronic transactions?

**2** What precautions should you take before purchasing from a website?

**3** Name three input and three output computer devices.

**4** For mobile work, what advantages does a PDA have compared with a laptop?

**5** Why might stored data be corrupted when an operating computer is moved?

**6** Name two types of computer virus.

**7** List the measures necessary to reduce the risk of computer virus infection.

**8** What basic precautions should be taken to restrict unauthorised access to computer data?

**9** Describe the purpose of the Data Protection Act.

**10** Name two government organisations that routinely exchange data.

**11** Explain how an intranet and an extranet might be used by an organisation.

**12** What steps can be taken to minimise the risk of purchasing pirated software?

**13** Explain the term asymmetric digital subscriber line (ADSL). What is the main benefit of ADSL when accessing the Internet from home?

**14** Name the most popular service available on the Internet.

E

# Section 2 *Multiple-choice questions*

**1** Which government agency should you seek advice from about the safe and responsible disposal of computer hardware?

 **a** Health.

 **b** Police.

 **c** Environment.

 **d** Fire.

**2** Which of the following date and time formats is standard in the USA?

 **a** DD/MM/YYYY.

 **b** MM/DD/YYYY.

 **c** YYYY/MM/DD.

 **d** YYYY/DD/MM.

**3** Which method is often employed by large organisations for backing up computer files?

 **a** Grandmother, mother, son.

 **b** Mother, auntie, niece.

 **c** Grandfather, father, son.

 **d** Father, uncle, nephew.

**4** Which Microsoft Office application offers the best facilities for sorting data?

 **a** Excel.

 **b** Word.

 **c** PowerPoint.

 **d** Access.

**5** The common text at the top and bottom of pages in a document is known as:

 **a** Mail merge.

 **b** Headers and footers.

 **c** Cut and paste.

 **d** Search and replace.

**6** Which of the following generic file formats is associated with spreadsheet applications?

**a** TXT.

**b** RTF.

**c** dif.

**d** csv.

**7** When copying/cutting and pasting between applications, data is stored in which area of memory?

**a** CD-ROM.

**b** Clipboard.

**c** Print buffer.

**d** Floppy disk.

**8** It would be most advantageous to hold an international computer qualification when:

**a** Moving within an organisation.

**b** Moving within the UK.

**c** Moving between countries.

**d** Moving between departments.

**9** In which of the following types of application would you most likely use Boolean logic functions?

**a** Database.

**b** Word processor.

**c** Desktop publishing.

**d** Presentation.

**10** Which type of computer uses the least energy?

**a** PDA.

**b** Desktop.

**c** Laptop.

**d** Mainframe.

E

**11**  The text used to correctly identify the data displayed on a chart is known as a:

    **a**  Logo.

    **b**  Header.

    **c**  Template.

    **d**  Legend.

**12**  A circular chart showing segments that are pulled apart is known as what?

    **a**  Pie.

    **b**  Bar.

    **c**  Column.

    **d**  Exploding pie.

**13**  Which of the following functions can help to minimise paper wastage?

    **a**  Screen saver.

    **b**  Print Preview.

    **c**  Copy and Paste.

    **d**  Mail Merge.

**14**  You might use a wildcard when:

    **a**  Searching for data.

    **b**  Entering a computer room.

    **c**  Backing up files.

    **d**  Using an ATM.

**15**  If you process and store information of a personal nature, you should register with the:

    **a**  National Police Database.

    **b**  Inland Revenue Service.

    **c**  Computer Misuse Commissioner.

    **d**  Data Protection Commissioner.

# Section 3  *Crossword*

**Across**

**4** Type of file that has the extension .exe (10)

**6** Try not to enter too many of these (6)

**7** Oldest backup version (11)

**9** Can help to visualise data (5)

**10** Common text at bottom of document (6)

**12** Part of a pie (7)

**14** Locations to hold data (5)

**15** Area of memory used when copying/cutting and pasting (9)

**16** You should do this to obsolete files (6)

**17** Can be accessed World Wide (3)

**Down**

**1** Farmers and database applications have them (6)

**2** Data sorted in date order (13)

**3** Link information between applications (5)

**5** Forbidden access (12)

**8** Style of text character (4)

**10** Can hold many files (6)

**11** Popular spreadsheet application (5)

**13** Often used with the cut function (5)